400 WOOD BOXES

The Fine Art of
Containment & Concealment

For Todd,

Thank you for the confidence
in my hands and spirit.

David O Kripfer

Ellicott City, MD

400 WOOD BOXES

The Fine Art of
Containment & Concealment

Introduction by
TONY LYDGATE

LARK BOOKS
A Division of Sterling Publishing Co., Inc.
New York

EDITOR
Veronika Alice Gunter

ART DIRECTOR
Celia Naranjo

PRODUCTION
Charlie Covington

COVER DESIGNER
Barbara Zaretsky

ASSISTANT EDITOR
Nathalie Mornu

EDITORIAL ASSISTANCE
Delores Gosnell
Jeff Hamilton
Rosemary Kast
Lorna Merry
Chelsea Pryor Wise

PRODUCTION ASSISTANCE
Shannon Yokeley

EDITORIAL INTERN
Rebecca Lim

ART INTERN
Laura Gabris

COVER IMAGE
John Mendez
Ornamental Box, 2002
Photo by Clifford Wheeler

TITLE PAGE IMAGE
Ervin Somogyi
Venere Shield, 1999
Photo by George Post

CONTENTS PAGE IMAGE
Jay Rogers
Opened Jewelry Box, 1999
Photo by Scott Chasteen

Library of Congress Cataloging-in-Publication Data

400 wood boxes : the fine art of containment & concealment / edited by Veronika Alice Gunter.-- 1st ed.
   p. cm.
  ISBN 1-57990-459-9 (pbk.)
  1. Woodwork. 2. Wooden boxes. I. Title: Four hundred wood boxes. II. Gunter, Veronika Alice.
  TT200.A18 2004
  684'.08--dc22

                                                    2003018513

10 9 8 7 6 5 4 3 2 1

First Edition

Published by Lark Books, a division of
Sterling Publishing Co., Inc.
387 Park Avenue South, New York, N.Y. 10016

© 2004, Lark Books

Distributed in Canada by Sterling Publishing,
c/o Canadian Manda Group, One Atlantic Ave., Suite 105
Toronto, Ontario, Canada M6K 3E7

Distributed in the U.K. by Guild of Master Craftsman Publications Ltd.,
Castle Place, 166 High Street, Lewes, East Sussex, England
BN7 1XU
Tel: (+ 44) 1273 477374, Fax: (+ 44) 1273 478606,
Email: pubs@thegmcgroup.com, Web: www.gmcpublications.com

Distributed in Australia by Capricorn Link (Australia) Pty Ltd.,
P.O. Box 704, Windsor, NSW 2756 Australia

The written instructions, photographs, designs, patterns, and projects in this volume are intended for the personal use of the reader and may be reproduced for that purpose only. Any other use, especially commercial use, is forbidden under law without written permission of the copyright holder.

Every effort has been made to ensure that all the information in this book is accurate. However, due to differing conditions, tools, and individual skills, the publisher cannot be responsible for any injuries, losses, and other damages that may result from the use of the information in this book.

If you have questions or comments about this book, please contact:
Lark Books
67 Broadway
Asheville, NC 28801
(828) 253-0467

Manufactured in China

ISBN 1-57990-459-9

CONTENTS

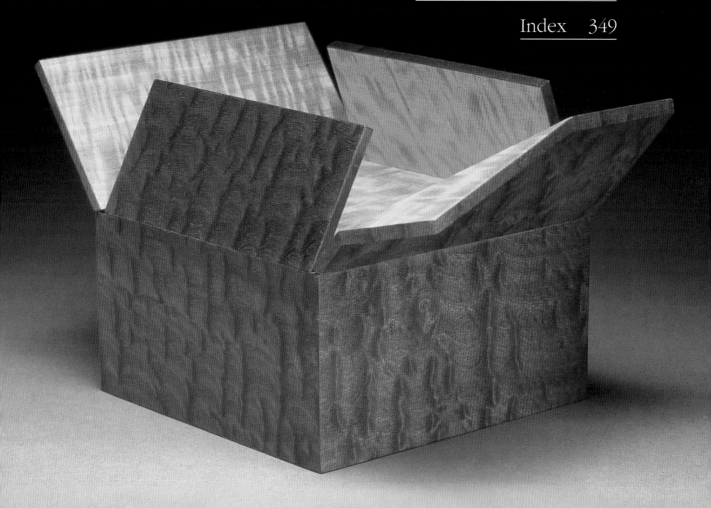

INTRODUCTION

In its essence, the wood box is a simple enough object—a container, often with four sides, a bottom, and a top that can be opened and closed. At the same time, the box is also a highly useful object, so much so that boxes have become among the most familiar, even commonplace items, in our everyday life.

Since the beginning of civilization, however, boxes have fascinated humankind, not for this usefulness, but because of the way the box seems to embrace that most human of all human qualities: contradiction. Like people, boxes do opposing things at the same time. On the one hand, the fundamental purpose of a box is to safeguard and protect its contents. It fulfills this purpose by removing those contents from sight, and hence from the harm that discovery might bring. Yet at the same time, by virtue of its very presence the box makes an announcement: I contain something valuable. In concealing, the box reveals.

To explore this contradiction, artists from at least as early as the time of the Egyptian Pharaohs have focused their creative efforts on the wood box, retaining its functionality while transforming its outward appearance according to their own artistic visions. New styles and ideas have influenced these visions over the generations, but all preserve the object's fundamental nature: a container, predominantly of wood, that can be opened and closed, and that reveals by hiding.

I have selected the boxes in this book to chronicle how today's boxmakers are continuing this tradition, and to showcase the astonishing variations they have invented on the theme of this apparently simple object. As you travel through these pages, you will see the extraordinarily diverse ways in which different makers have chosen tools and techniques, forms and shapes, materials and aesthetic approaches to create boxes that embody their own beliefs about what is beautiful.

The majority of the designs in this book are intended for tabletop display, but a number of makers have adapted their boxes to serve as wall cabinets, freestanding pieces, or chests to be set on the floor. Some have followed tradition in choosing the rectangle as the basis for the proportional dimensions of length, width, and height. Others have pushed traditional boundaries by creating variations on the theme of conventional shape, and not a few have discarded conventional shape altogether to make unusual and unique forms.

These boxes vary widely in their use, from the purely sculptural to the strictly utilitarian. New designs for practical containers—silver chests, lap desks, cigar humidors, and boxes to hold chess sets—are found alongside sculptural containers so beautiful as objects in themselves that whether they are useful for holding anything seems beside the point.

All the traditional woodworking techniques are represented here, including joinery, carving, marquetry and inlay, lamination, and lathe-turning. A number of designs combine techniques, by adding carving to joinery, for example, or lathe-turning a lamination.

Although each box is made predominantly from wood, materials such as metal, plastic resin, glass, and even found objects also appear, often in unexpected combinations. A wide range is also evident in choice of finish or surface treatment. Some boxmakers emphasize the beauty of highly figured wood, freeing it from bark-covered darkness to show its natural color, and bringing out its grain patterns with clear finishes, frequently given a high polish. Others deliberately avoid this familiar high-polish, exotic wood convention, preferring finishes that decorate the wood with pigment, burning, or non-wood materials, or even cover it completely with paint.

Finally, some designs tell you that a maker feels great reverence for a traditional form; in contrast, others seem playful, even tongue-in-cheek. Every box will invite you as the viewer to form an impression of the boxmaker's attitude toward the work, and you will find it interesting to contrast the ways in which some designs pay deliberate homage to well-known woodworking ideals, while others make a wry comment on the risks of taking yourself too seriously.

Whichever ones become your favorites, the designs in this book make it clear that still today, thousands of years after its first ancestor was fashioned, the wood box continues to fascinate, surprise, and inspire.

Tony Lydgate

PETER F. DELLERT
Atlantis, 2001
20¼"H x 20¼"W x 4"D (51 x 51 x 10 CM)
Mahogany, mixed-media collage, vintage
glass lens
PHOTOS BY JOHN POLAK

PETER F. DELLERT
Shooting Stars II, 2000
31½"H x 16"W x 8"D
(80 x 41 x 20 CM)
Ash, copper, cherry
PHOTOS BY JOHN POLAK

9

MICHAEL UNCAPHER

MICHAEL UNCAPHER
A.J., 1998
21½"H X 7"W X 8"D (55 X 18 X 20 CM)
Wenge, holly
PHOTO BY PIPER STUDIO

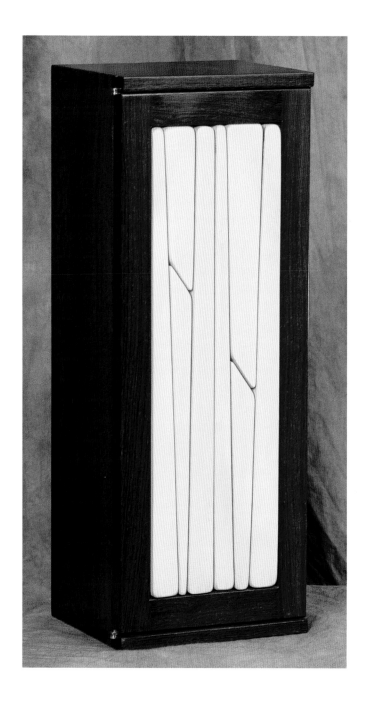

JOHN MENDEZ
Ornamental Box, 2002
8"H X 4½"W X 4½"D
(20 X 11 X 11 CM)
Maple, padauk, cherry,
turquoise
PHOTO BY CLIFFORD WHEELER

JOHN MENDEZ
Haida Bear Box, 1997
9"H x 12"W x 8"D (23 x 31 x 20 CM)
Walnut, cherry
PHOTO BY CLIFFORD WHEELER

JOHN MENDEZ
Bear Cub Box, 2001
6"H X 12"W X 4"D (15 X 30 X 10 CM)
Walnut, zebrawood
PHOTO BY ARTIST

Carved bear cub handle;
mitered and pinned lid;
finger jointed box and tray

MATTHEW R. JOPPICH

MATTHEW R. JOPPICH
Wiseman's Box, 2002
3"H X 8"W X 5"D (8 X 20 X 13 CM)
Bay laurel, yellow cedar
PHOTO BY DON RUTT PHOTOGRAPHY

SETH A. BARRETT

SETH A. BARRETT
Jewelry Box, 2002
24"H x 22"W x 14"D (61 x 56 x 36 CM)
Maple, curly maple, flame birch, purpleheart
PHOTOS BY FRANK IANNOTTI

SETH A. BARRETT
Untitled, 1999
33"H X 24"W X 14"D (84 X 61 X 36 CM)
Mahogany, ash, walnut, poplar
PHOTO BY FRANK IANNOTTI

SETH A. BARRETT
Cabinet Structure, 1999
84"H X 21"W X 21"D (213 X 53 X 53 CM)
Walnut, beech, zebrawood
PHOTO BY FRANK IANNOTTI

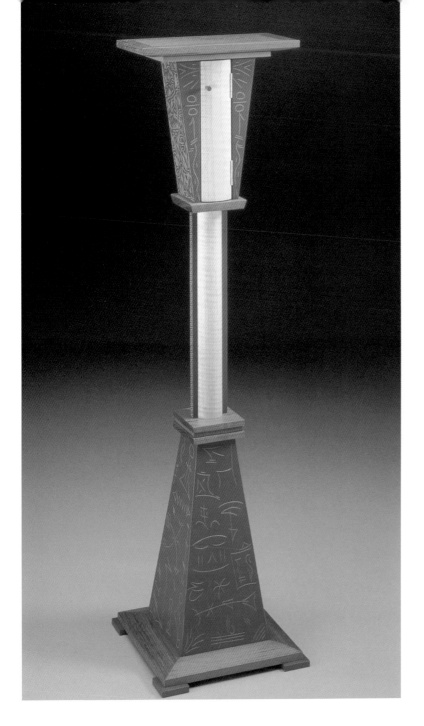

MARK DEL GUIDICE
Pedestal Box, 2000
43"H X 12"W X 11"D (109 X 31 X 28 CM)
Madrone burl, jatoba, basswood, curly maple
PHOTO BY DEAN POWELL

*This form was based on Egyptian amulets.
It was finished with milk paint and
signature hieroglyphs.*

MARK DEL GUIDICE
As Luck Would Have It (jewelry box stand), 2001
46"H X 18"W X 11"D (117 X 46 X 28 CM)
Bird's-eye maple, walnut, basswood, mirror, leather
PHOTOS BY DEAN POWELL

MARK DEL GUIDICE
Chest of Treasure, 2003
15"H X 22"W X 16"D (38 X 56 X 41 CM)
Figured bubinga, walnut, pear
PHOTOS BY CLEMENTS/HOWCROFT

The carved Morse code reads "Chest of Treasure."

BRIAN MCLACHLAN
Heartland Box, 1999
9"H x 17"W x 15"D (23 x 43 x 38 CM)
Mesquite, curly maple, ebony, yellowheart, redheart, padauk, teak, ash
PHOTOS BY RAY BALLHEIM AND BILL ALBRECHT

WAYNE AND LINDA HONER
Power of the Pyramid, 2002
10"H x 14"W x 14" D (25 x 36 x 36 CM)
Walnut, spalted maple

PHOTOS BY SALLY ANN PHOTOGRAPHY

The velvet-lined compartments of this five-tier pyramid open by sliding and rotation. The box features mitered and slipfeathered joints.

WAYNE AND LINDA HONER
Violin Jewelry Keepsake, 2001
2¾"H x 17"W x 7"D
(7 x 43 x 18 CM)
Spalted maple, walnut, bocote,
brass, ebony
PHOTO BY SALLY ANN PHOTOGRAPHY

M. THOMAS DEAN
Curly Tiger Box, 2003
3"H X 11"W X 7½"D (8 X 28 X 19 CM)
Curly maple, myrtle burl, redheart
PHOTOS BY JOSTEN'S PHOTOGRAPHY

JONATHAN DER
Small Tansu, 2000
13"H x 22"W x 12"D (33 x 56 x 31 CM)
Walnut, white oak, maple
PHOTO BY HAP SAKWA

The four-way book match was cut from a scrap of crotch walnut and veneered to the drawer fronts.

GARY SANDERS
Spirit in the Sky, 2003
3"H X 10"W X 5"D
(8 X 25 X 13 CM)
Cocobolo, box elder burl
PHOTO BY ARTIST

GARY SANDERS
*Snake Charmer's
Basket,* 2003
3"H X 10"W X 5"D
(8 X 25 X 13 CM)
Cocobolo, box elder burl
PHOTO BY ARTIST

MICHAEL HAMILTON &
DEE ROBERTS

**MICHAEL HAMILTON AND
DEE ROBERTS**
Reliquary, 2002
9"H X 8"W X 5½"D
(23 X 20 X 14 CM)
Beeswing eucalyptus, cocobolo
rosewood, ebony, sterling silver
PHOTOS BY GEORGE POST

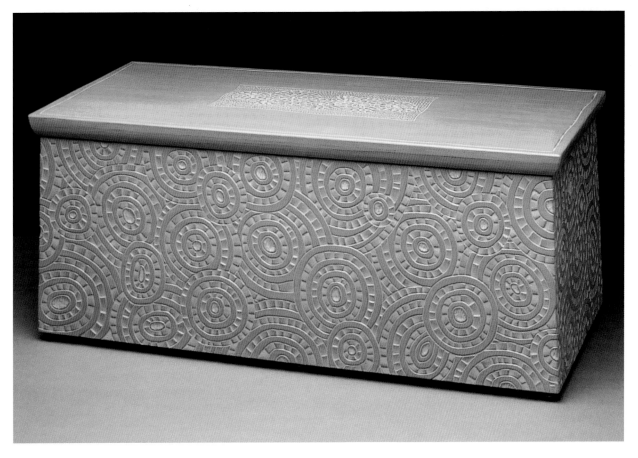

MICHAEL CULLEN
Snowflake Chest, 2000
10"H X 22"W X 9½"D (25 X 56 X 24 CM)
Mahogany, nutmeg
PHOTO BY DON RUSSELL

Hand-carved mahogany body with spines at mitered joints, nutmeg interior bottom, and milk paint finish

MICHAEL CULLEN
Elephant Chest, 2000
11"H x 16"W x 10"D (28 x 41 x 25 CM)
Mahogany, redwood burl
PHOTO BY JOHN MCDONALD

"Boxes and chests are perhaps my favorite objects to design and make: they allow me the opportunity to create an intimate space for treasure."

MICHAEL CULLEN
Leaf Jewelry Chest, 2002
14"H X 20"W X 12½"D (36 X 51 X 32 CM)
Pear, curly maple, cocobolo, ebony
PHOTO BY JOHN MCDONALD

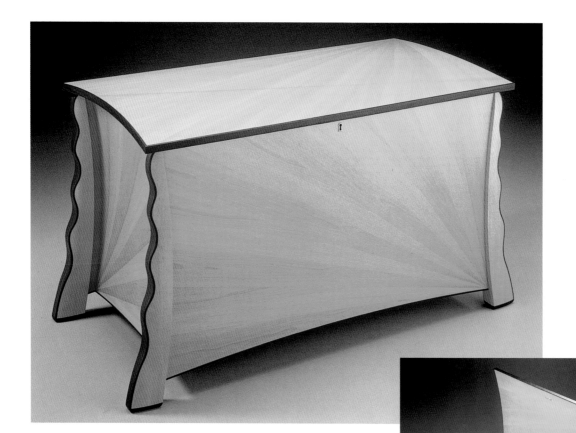

JAMIE ROBERTSON
Lemonwood Chest, 1997
24"H x 46"W x 22"D (61 x 117 x 56 CM)
Lemonwood, Indian rosewood, pau amarello,
cedar, birch
PHOTOS BY DEAN POWELL

JAMIE ROBERTSON

*"This is a chest that you could take
with you on a long voyage."*

MICHAEL WERNER
Hot Coffee, 2002
9"H X 5¾"W X 5¼"D (23 X 15 X 13 CM)
Russian olive, padauk, walnut, wire
PHOTOS BY ARTIST

The cup and saucer are turned endgrain from a log with natural edge. The steam is made of aluminum wire.

MICHAEL WERNER
…In the Yellow Submarine, 2002
4"H x 4½"W x 8"D (10 x 11 x 20 CM)
Fir, poplar, maple, aluminum
PHOTOS BY ARTIST

The eggshell mosaic design consists of tiny pieces of eggshell, painted with custom-mixed enamels, hand-applied to the box with watchmaker's tweezers.

SHERRI LINDSAY
Saturday Evening, 2003
7"H x 5½"W x 4½"D (18 x 14 x 11 CM)
Poplar, eggshell
PHOTOS BY HAP SAKWA

ALAN G. KAPLAN

ALAN G. KAPLAN
*Horizontal Bud-Vase Box
with Bud Vase,* 2003
6"H x 16"W x 3½"D
(15 x 41 x 9 CM)
Cherry, sycamore, bubinga,
glass
PHOTOS BY ELLEN MARTIN

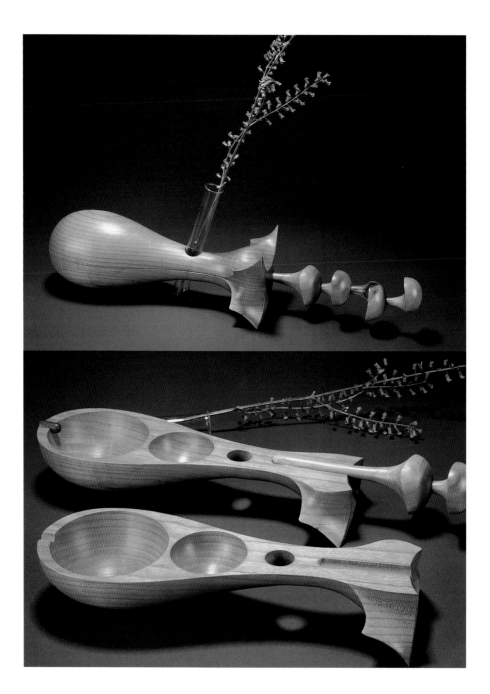

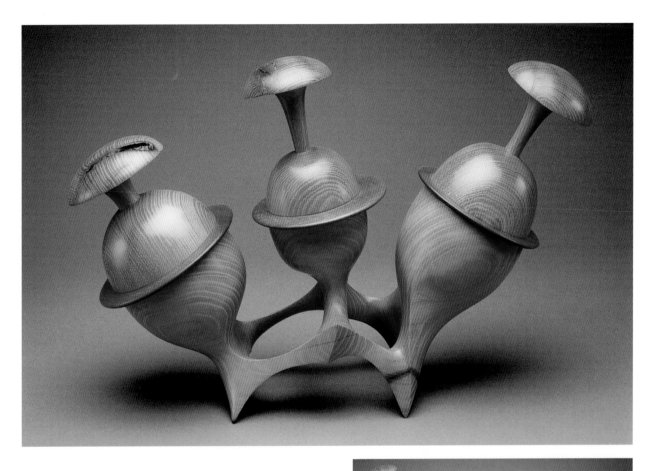

Alan G. Kaplan
Three Ring Circus, 2003
10"H x 12"W x 3½"D (25 x 31 x 9 cm)
Osage orange, mahogany
PHOTOS BY ELLEN MARTIN

*Lathe-turned using multi-axis
technique, hard carved*

DAVRILL NASH
Jewelry Box, 2003
4"H x 14"W x 8"D (10 x 36 x 20 CM)
Maple, cherry
PHOTO BY PRR ASS

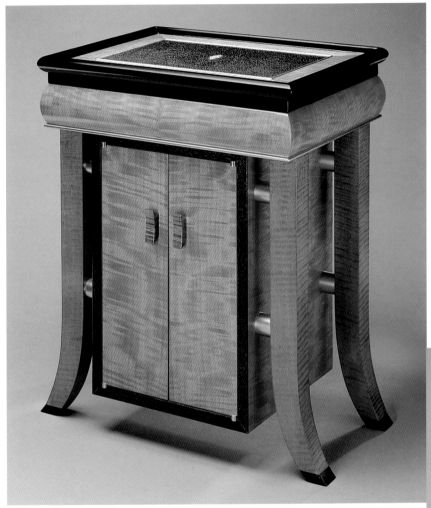

CARL TESE
Temple, 2001
20"H X 14"W X 12"D (51 X 36 X 31 CM)
Block mottled anigre, curly maple, bird's-eye maple, stingray leather
PHOTOS BY JEFF WATTS

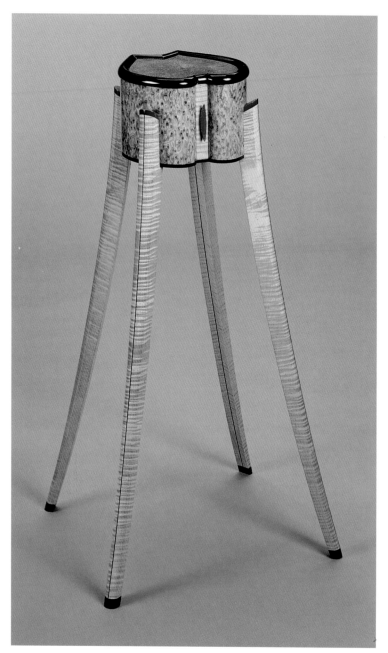

CARL TESE
Modus Tollens, 2002
39"H x 24"W x 20"D (99 x 61 x 51 CM)
Curly maple, bird's-eye maple, curly anigre,
purpleheart, stingray leather
PHOTOS BY RAFFI

CARL TESE
Logical Analogy, 2000
8"H x 19"W x 8"D (20 x 48 x 20 CM)
Quilted maple, curly maple, bird's-eye
maple, purpleheart, fabric
PHOTO BY JEFF WATTS

JOHN BURKE
Jewel Box, 2001
5"H x 4½"W x 2½"D (13 x 11 x 6 CM)
Yew, maple
PHOTOS BY ANDREW CRAWFORD

MICHAEL LOW
Volcano Box, 2003
5"H X 12"W X 8"D
(13 X 31 X 20 CM)
China berry wood, curly
maple, cocobolo, leather
PHOTO BY ARTIST

FRANÇOIS MASSÉ
Nancy's Box, 2002
2⅝"H X 13⅝"W X 6⅜"D
(7 X 35 X 16 CM)
Douglas fir, cherry, kinwashi paper,
unryu paper, lime, Gabon ebony,
Nepali paper, brass, cord
PHOTO BY ARTIST

A box for love letters

RAY JONES

RAY JONES
Hang 'em High II, 2002
14"H x 9"W x 11"D
(36 x 23 x 28 CM)
Okoume, ebony, avodire
PHOTOS BY TIM BARNWELL

RAY JONES
We Come in Peace, 2001
8"H X 12"W X 12"D (20 X 31 X 31 CM)
Mahogany, ebony, avodire
PHOTOS BY TIM BARNWELL

This box has 23 turned components.

43

RAY JONES
Bull's-Eye, 2002
19"H x 18"W x 10"D (48 x 46 x 25 CM)
Mahogany, ebony, avodire
PHOTOS BY TIM BARNWELL

The artist was trained as an aerospace engineer. Since 1982 he has made a living by designing, making, and selling wood boxes. "I love my job!"

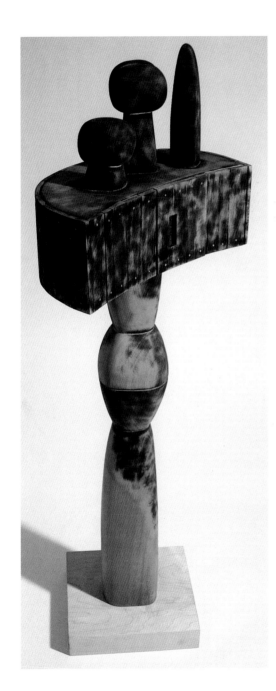

JEREMY COMINS
Secret Place, 2002
36"H X 11"W X 7"D
(92 X 28 X 18 CM)
Mahogany, nailed planking
PHOTO BY ARTIST

EMIL FRIEDMAN
Untitled, 2000
4¼"H X 6"W X 3¾"D
(11 X 15 X 10 CM)
Mahogany, oak, walnut,
brass, saxophone reeds
PHOTO BY JEREMY COMINS

BILL KIMBELL
Flower Jewelry Box, 2002
3"H X 7"W X 12"D (8 X 18 X 31 CM)
Crotch walnut, padauk, bubinga, Indian rosewood,
sycamore, mouingui
PHOTO BY ARTIST

BILL KIMBELL

BILL KIMBELL

Tiger Jewelry Box, 2003

3¼"H x 12"w x 6¼"D (8 x 31 x 16 cm)

Curly koa, mahogany, mappa burl, maple burl, ebony, aspen, curly maple, koa, walnut

PHOTOS BY ARTIST

JOHN A. MCDERMOTT

JOHN A. MCDERMOTT
Bandsaw Box, 2002
5"H X 3½"W X 18"D (13 X 9 X 46 CM)
Black walnut
PHOTOS BY MARTIN FOX

JACK JACKSON

Pedestal Box, 2002

14¼"H X 12½"W X 6½"D
(36 X 32 X 17 CM)

Walnut, bird's-eye maple,
brass hooks

PHOTOS BY GEOFFREY CARR

JACK JACKSON

JACK JACKSON

Pedestal Box, 2002

14¼"H X 12½"W X 6½"D
(36 X 32 X 17 CM)

Lacewood, cherry, brass hooks

PHOTO BY GEOFFREY CARR

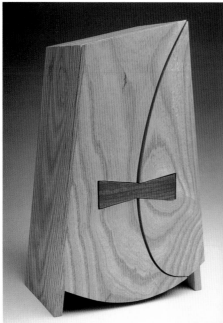

SETH ROLLAND
Bowtie Box, 1997
17"H x 10"W x 7"D (43 x 25 x 18 CM)
White ash, padauk
PHOTOS BY PAT POLLARD

SETH ROLLAND

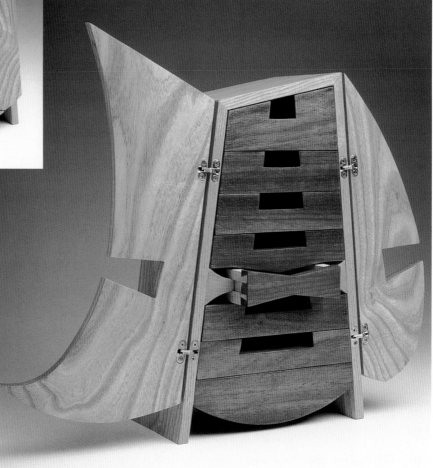

"Small boxes are like sketches: they allow me to try out new ideas before incorporating them in larger pieces of furniture."

SETH ROLLAND
Barbed Box, 1996
9"H x 9"W x 5"D (23 x 23 x 13 CM)
Poplar, barbed wire, pennies
PHOTO BY PAT POLLARD

EVAN COST

EVAN COST
The Rotten Box, 2000
8"H X 15½"W X 11½"D (21 X 40 X 29 CM)
Curly spalted maple, ebony, brass hinges
PHOTO BY MAGGIE WOCHELE

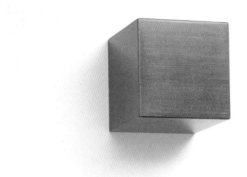

CARLO MARCUCCI
Wheatfields V, 1996
28"H X 28"W X 7"D
(71 X 71 X 18 CM)
PLUS 7" CUBE (18 CM)
Birch, Italian and Japanese
rice, wheat spaghetti

*"These minimal compositions are
abstract interpretations of food
containers and the disproportionate role
they have in processed food distribution.
In a metaphorical sense, the box
containing the spaghetti is reborn as a
box constructed of spaghetti."*

Collection of Littler and Mendelson

53

JOHN POLLOCK

JOHN POLLOCK
Untitled, 2002
5"H X 9"W X 5"D (13 X 23 X 13 CM)
Buckeye burl
PHOTO BY ARTIST

*Natural edge, bandsawed puzzle box with a
drawer and a hidden compartment*

JOHN POLLOCK
Untitled, 2002
7"H x 19"W x 11½"D
(18 x 48 x 29 CM)
Claro walnut burl, mahogany
PHOTO BY ARTIST

*Sculpted, bandsawed puzzle box
with multiple trays, drawers, and
compartments—several of which
are hidden*

JOHN POLLOCK
Untitled, 2002
5"H x 14"W x 7"D (13 x 36 x 18 CM)
Claro walnut burl, black walnut
PHOTO BY ARTIST

ROBERT LaBONTE

ROBERT LaBONTE
Bombé Box, 2003
5"H x 9"W x 5"D (13 x 23 x 13 CM)
Australian lacewood, wenge, ebony
PHOTO BY DAVID CUMPSTON

The curved sides highlight the figure of the lacewood.

ROBERT LaBONTE
Zig Zag Box, 2003
6"H x 6"W x 3"D (15 x 15 x 8 CM)
Walnut, cocobolo, African blackwood
PHOTO BY DAVID CUMPSTON

"This box was inspired by the way a potter would make a box: slabs stuck together. Bookmatching the front and back was the right thing to do! The hollow lid is for surprise."

JEFFERY MEEUWSEN

JEFFERY MEEUWSEN
Classified, 2002
30"H x 14"W x 20"D (76 x 36 x 51 CM)
Mahogany, found objects
PHOTO BY CHUCK HEINEY

*Courtesy of
Kendall College of
Art and Design*

PETER LLOYD

Chess Box, 2001

18"H x 10"W x 6"D (45 x 25 x 15 CM)

Ripple sycamore, American black walnut, box-wood, ebony, leather

PHOTOS BY ARTIST

59

PETER LLOYD
Stationery Box, 2001
16"H x 12"W x 6"D (40 x 30 x 15 CM)
Tiger oak, leather
PHOTOS BY ARTIST

PETER LLOYD
Crease, 2003
30"H x 20"W x 12"D
(76 x 51 x 31 CM)
PHOTO BY ARTIST

STEVEN LACKO
MeGhann, 1995
3"H x 9"W x 3½"D (8 x 23 x 9 CM)
Cherry, velvet
PHOTO BY JOHN KORNICK

61

GENE KANGAS

GENE KANGAS
Birthday Cake Box, 1998
8"H X 20"D (20 X 51 CM)
PHOTOS BY ARTIST

This large turned and highly decorated box is a sculpture with a serious message about drunk driving.

GENE KANGAS
Melon Box, 1997
7"H x 15½"D (18 x 39 CM)
Mahogany, maple, poplar
PHOTOS BY ARTIST

GENE KANGAS
Coffee Cup Box, 1997
10"H X 17"D (25 X 43 CM)
Mahogany, walnut, maple
PHOTOS BY ARTIST

*The oversized coffee cup has a unique lid and handle
for opening the box: you hold the spoon as if you were
going to stir the coffee to lift out the lid.*

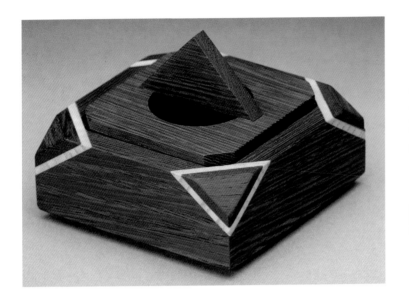

ANDY VAN DER TUIN
5 Triangle Box, 2003
3"H x 3¾"W x 3¾"D (8 x 10 x 10 CM)
Wenge, ash
PHOTO BY LON BRAUER

ANDY VAN DER TUIN

ANDY VAN DER TUIN
F.D.R. Series, 2003
2½"H x 3¾"W x 3¾"D TO
2¼"H x 7½"W x 3¾"D
(6 x 10 x 10 CM TO
6 x 19 x 10 CM)
Cherry, maple, wenge, mahogany
PHOTO BY LON BRAUER

*Each handle has a small piece of
mahogany that came from a drawer
front of a desk once owned by
President Franklin D. Roosevelt.*

ANDY VAN DER TUIN
Pyramid Box, 2003
2¾"H X 7½"W X 3¾"D (7 X 19 X 10 CM)
Cherry, ash, wenge, canary wood, redheart
PHOTO BY LON BRAUER

ROBERT SVERDUK
Display Case, 2001
6½"H x 14"W x 9"D (17 x 36 x 23 CM)
Maple
PHOTO BY ARTIST

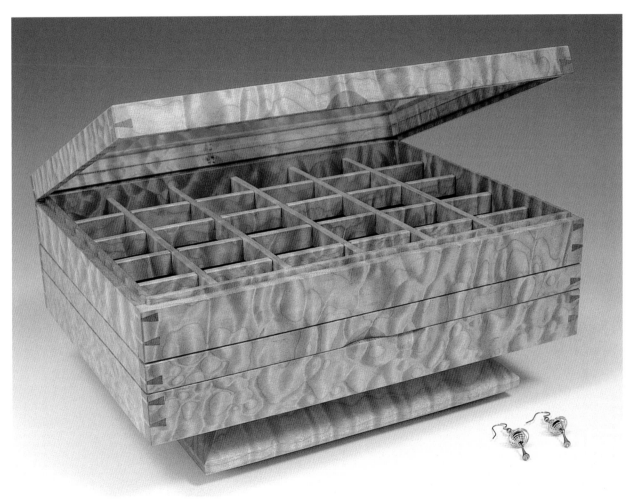

ROBERT SVERDUK
Spiral Jewelry Box, 2003
14"H X 8"W X 8"D
(36 X 20 X 20 CM)
Gabon ebony, holly, brass
PHOTO BY ARTIST

ROBERT SVERDUK
*Pentagonal Geometric
Jewelry Box,* 2003
7"H X 9"D (18 X 23 CM)
Bocote, aromatic cedar,
American holly
PHOTO BY ARTIST

ALAN BRADSTREET
Lizard Box, 1997
2¼"H x 7½"w x 5"D (6 x 19 x 13 CM)
Walnut, ash
PHOTO BY DENNIS GRIGGS

ALAN BRADSTREET

Carpenter Ant Box, 1994

5"H X 6½"W X 3½"D (13 X 17 X 9 CM)

Cherry, walnut, ash, copper wire, aluminum

PHOTO BY DENNIS GRIGGS

"My boxes generally reflect designs from nature. They often incorporate humor and unusual twists, including transformations from two to three dimensions and other surprises inside the box."

JEFFERY B. SCHWARM
Mahogany Moab, 2002
6"H x 15"W x 10¾"D (15 x 38 x 28 CM)
Mahogany, figured maple, brass, velvet
PHOTO BY JERRY ANTHONY PHOTOGRAPHY

JEFFERY B. SCHWARM

JEFFERY B. SCHWARM
Double Duty, 2003
8¼"H x 15½"W x 11½"D (21 x 40 x 29 CM)
Red oak, walnut, brass, velvet
PHOTO BY JERRY ANTHONY PHOTOGRAPHY

KURT ALLEN
*Jewelry Box with Ball
and Claw Feet,* 2002
8"H x 13"W x 10"D
(21 x 33 x 26 CM)
Cherry, curly cherry,
madrone burl, ebony,
fiddleback maple
PHOTO BY
GIANLUCA CASAGRANDE

ELIZABETH WHITELEY

ELIZABETH WHITELEY
Wood Form I, 2000
4"H x 8½"W x 6½"D
(10 x 22 x 17 cm)
Tiger maple
PHOTOS BY ARTIST

ELIZABETH WHITELEY
Wood Form II, 2000
3½"H x 8½"W x 8½"D (9 x 22 x 22 CM)
Tiger maple, cherry
PHOTO BY ARTIST

NICOLA HENSHAW

NICOLA HENSHAW
*Egret, Wagtail, and
Snipe Boxes,* 2000
EGRET: 20"H X 8"W X 16"D
(51 X 20 X 41 CM)
WAGTAIL: 14"H X 8"W X 18"D
(36 X 20 X 46 CM)
SNIPE: 9"H X 8"W X 16"D
(23 X 20 X 41 CM)
Oak, lime wood
PHOTO BY ANDRA NELKI

NICOLA HENSHAW
Pelican Box, 1999
25"H X 10"W X 10"D
(64 X 25 X 25 CM)
Redwood
PHOTO BY ANDRA NELKI

NICOLA HENSHAW
*Wader Box with Fish
Inside,* 2002
16"H X 10"W X 14"D
(41 X 25 X 36 CM)
Oak, lime
PHOTO BY MARK CURZON

RON LOWE

RON LOWE
Curio, 2002
19¾"H X 11½"W X 7½"D (50 X 27 X 19 CM)
Nogal, spalted maple, maple
PHOTOS BY ARTIST

RON LOWE
A Work of Arches, 2002
3¼"H x 6¼"W x 4¾"D
(9 x 16 x 12 CM)
Ebonized wenge
PHOTOS BY ARTIST

*This box is based on the square
root of the number two.*

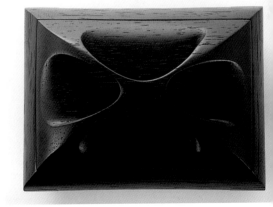

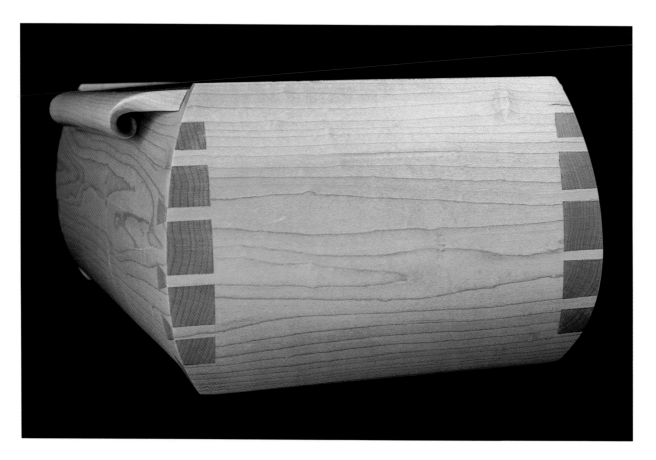

RON LOWE
Summerhill Wine Box, 2002
2"H x 8"W x 3¾"D (5 x 20 x 9 CM)
Walnut, olive, pernambuco
PHOTOS BY VINCENT MCDONALD

DEWEY GARRETT
Orb Box, 1996
6"H x 6"W x 6"D (15 x 15 x 15 CM)
Oak, walnut
PHOTOS BY ARTIST

DEWEY GARRETT
Cosmos, 2000
3½"H x 8"W x 8"D (9 x 20 x 20 CM)
Peroba, chakte kok
PHOTOS BY ARTIST

HILARY ARNOLD-BAKER
Sheltered, 2003
5 x 16 x 9
Pine, driftwood, gesso, gold leaf
PHOTO BY JAMES ARNOLD-BAKER

HILARY ARNOLD-BAKER
Lapis Lazuli Box, 2000
2"H X 6"W X 4"D (5 X 16 X 9 CM)
Pine, mixed media, gold leaf
PHOTO BY JAMES ARNOLD-BAKER

*Trompe l'oeil lapis lazuli with gilded raised gesso
bindings. Support is gilded driftwood nest*

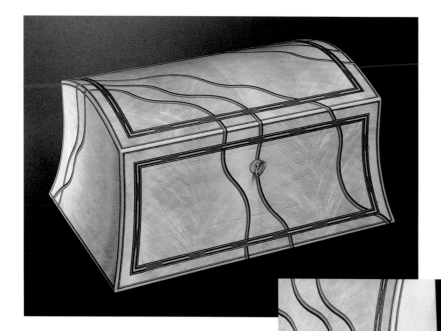

ANDREW CRAWFORD

ANDREW CRAWFORD
*Large Curved Form
Jewelry Box,* 1999
18"H X 10"W X 8"D
(46 X 25 X 20 CM)
Birch, rock maple, burr
maple, mother of pearl
PHOTOS BY ARTIST

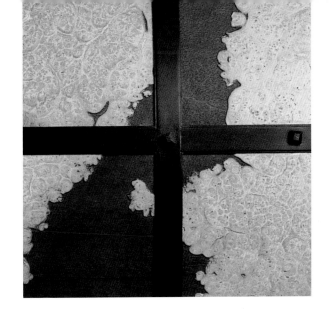

ANDREW CRAWFORD
Treasure Island, 1999
15"H X 10"W X 8"D (38 X 25 X 20 CM)
Birch, amboyna, ebony
PHOTO BY ARTIST

PHILLIP THIBODEAU
Surfer Dude, 2003
5¼"H x 8½"w x 5"D (13 x 22 x 13 CM)
Walnut, cherry, cocobolo
PHOTO BY BOB PURLA COMMERCIAL PHOTOGRAPHY

Phillip Thibodeau
FXRS, 2003
5"H x 9"W x 4½"D (13 x 23 x 12 cm)
Walnut, cherry, cocobolo
PHOTO BY BOB PURLA COMMERCIAL PHOTOGRAPHY

PHILLIP THIBODEAU
Toadstool, 2002
5½"H X 9"W X 5"D (14 X 23 X 13 CM)
Cherry, cocobolo
PHOTO BY ARTIST

"The idea for doing the Toadstool *box came in a flash of inspiration while raking my yard. I was struck by the organic symmetry of the mushrooms and toadstools growing under a cluster of pine trees."*

CINDY DROZDA
Jarrah Burl and Blackwood Container, 2003
4¼"H x 5¾"W x 5¾"D (11 x 14 x 14 CM)
Jarrah, African blackwood, 23k gold leaf, gold
and rhodium bead
PHOTOS BY TIM BENKO/BENKO PHOTOGRAPHICS

CINDY DROZDA
Space Station
(oval lidded container), 2002
4½"H X 3½"W X 3½"D
(11 X 9 X 9 CM)
Bamksia seed pod, 23k gold leaf
PHOTO BY TIM BENKO/BENKO
PHOTOGRAPHICS

*Lathe turned from a
single bamksia seed pod.
The holes in the pod are
where the seeds were.*

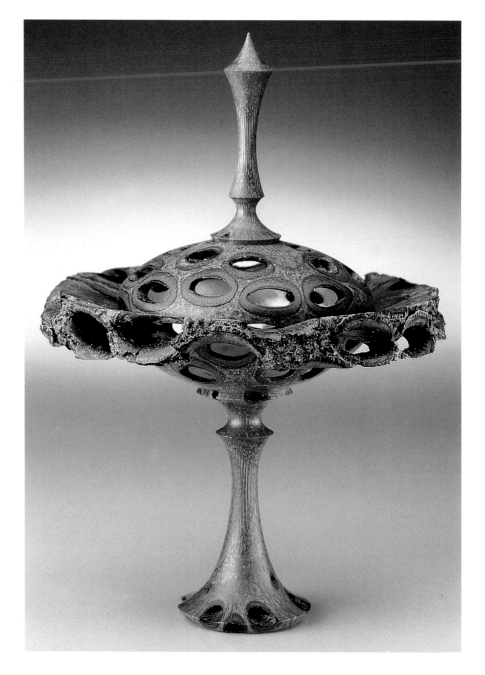

DAVID CHARLES KNIPFER
Soaring, 2003
22"H x 11"W x 6"D (56 x 28 x 15 CM)
Cherry, walnut, velvet
PHOTOS BY DAVID EGAN PHOTOGRAPHY

DAVID CHARLES KNIPFER
Pisces, 2003
15"H X 9"W X 7"D (38 X 23 X 18 CM)
Cherry, satinwood, purpleheart, velvet
PHOTO BY DAVID EGAN PHOTOGRAPHY

*"This box is named for the shape of
the pulls. Making them is a fun way to
spend some time when the remainder
of the household has gone to bed."*

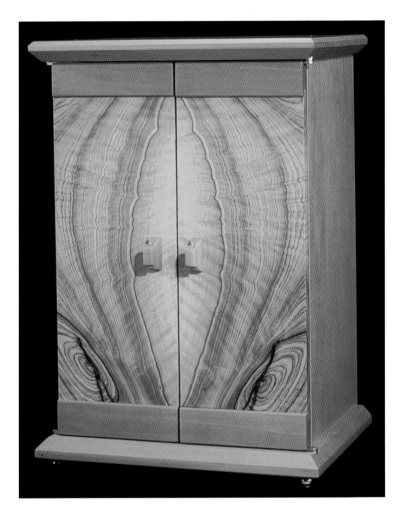

DAVID CHARLES KNIPFER
Starburst, 2002
15"H X 11"W X 7"D (38 X 28 X 18 CM)
Swiss pear, curly olive, wenge, maple, velvet
PHOTOS BY DAVID EGAN PHOTOGRAPHY

"The lovely curly olive bookmatched door panels in this box were the inspiration for the design: I built the box to showcase this once-in-a-lifetime piece of wood. How I wish I could find more olive just like this piece!"

The rich, black color of wenge creates a contrast when you open the doors of Starburst. *The strips of olive used as the pulls bring your attention back to the doors.*

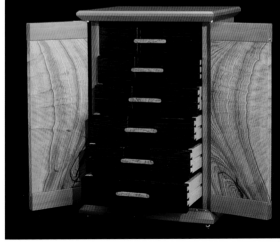

JIM CHRISTIANSEN
Nakisha's Treasure, 2000
12½"H x 5"W (32 x 13 CM)
Maple burl
PHOTOS BY WILL SIMPSON

This box represents an effort to show that wood art comes from the earth. "All creation is related to natural processes of birth, growth, death, renewal."

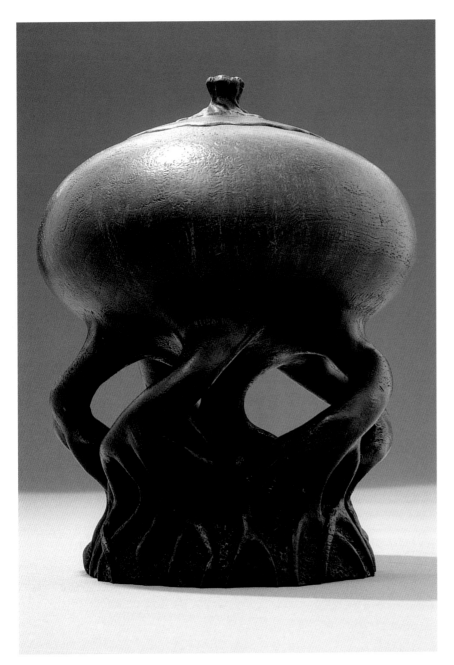

JIM CHRISTIANSEN
Twisted Truth, 2003
6¼"H x 4½"W (16 x 11 CM)
Black locust burl
PHOTOS BY WILL SIMPSON

JIM CHRISTIANSEN
Protobird II, 2002
3¾"H x 5⅞"W (10 x 15 CM)
Maple, box elder
PHOTOS BY WILL SIMPSON

THOMAS CLARK
Mahogany Humidor, 2002
7"H x 13½"W x 9"D (18 x 35 x 23 cm)
Mahogany, wenge
PHOTO BY TIM WILSON

MATT HUTTON

MATT HUTTON
Secret Safe, 2000
52"H x 41"W x 19"D (132 x 104 x 48 CM)
Mahogany, maple, leather, mirror
PHOTOS BY MICHAELJAMESIMAGE.COM

MATT HUTTON
3 Door Cabinet, 2001
54"H x 12"W x 12"D (137 x 31 x 31 CM)
Mahogany, limba

PHOTOS BY MICHAELJAMESIMAGE.COM

BRENDA BEHRENS
Treasures Within Protected by Snake Fetish, 1997
8"H X 6½"W X 6½"D
(21 X 17 X 17 CM)
Rosewood, padauk, mahogany, walnut, maple, purpleheart, horse hair, pheasant feathers, shell beads
PHOTO BY ARTIST

BRENDA BEHRENS

BRENDA BEHRENS
Footed Leaf Box, 1999
3"H X 8"W X 8"D (8 X 21 X 21 CM)
Figured myrtle
PHOTO BY ARTIST

KIM KELZER
Nesting Boxes (group of five), 2002
7¼"H x 6"w x 6½"D (18 x 15 x 17 cm) TO
1½"H x 1¼"w x 1"D (4 x 3 x 3 cm)
Mahogany
PHOTO BY RACHEL OLSSON

Bandsawed boxes from one chunk of mahogany

ROBERT PICOU

ROBERT PICOU
Untitled, 2003
4½"H x 15"w x 9"D
(11 x 38 x 23 cm)
New England tiger maple, walnut,
snakewood, ebony, holly, brass
PHOTO BY CHARLES BUSH AND ERIC PITRE

101

PHOTO BY SARA MORRIS

The twist is machined into the solid timber using complex jigs to achieve an accuracy that allows the box lid to sit flush in all four positions.

SARAH KAY

SARAH KAY
Torque Box, 2000
9"H x 6"W x 6"D (22 x 15 x 15 CM)
Hardwoods
PHOTO BY SARA MORRIS

JEFFREY REYNOLDS
Humidor, 2003
5"H x 12½"W x 9½"D (13 x 32 x 24 CM)
Lacewood, wenge, Spanish cedar
PHOTOS BY LARRY M. BUTLER

STEVEN B. LEVINE
Wings, 1998
8"H x 21"W x 14"D
(20 x 53 x 36 CM)
Olive-ash burl, purpleheart,
maple, suede
PHOTO BY GRANT PETERSON

STEVEN B. LEVINE
Slant, 2001
Cherry, ebony, holly, mirror
PHOTO BY GRANT PETERSON

STEVEN B. LEVINE
Stacking Jewelry Box, 2002
Bubinga, ebony, holly
PHOTO BY GRANT PETERSON

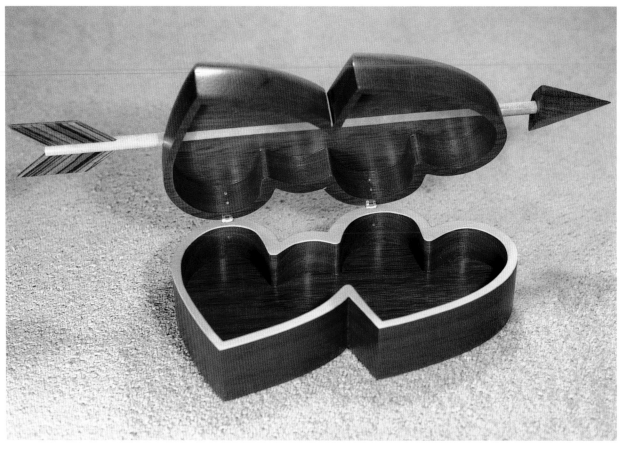

RICHARD W. GOEBEL

RICHARD W. GOEBEL
Double Heart, 2002
3"H x 18"W x 7"D (8 x 46 x 18 CM)
Purpleheart, holly, birch, walnut, zebrano
PHOTOS BY FRED J. GOEBEL

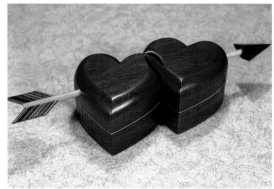

**DOUGLAS W. JONES AND
KIM KULOW-JONES**
Ring Box, 2002
8"H x 4½"D (20 x 11 CM)
Mahogany
PHOTO BY JERRY ANTHONY

*Lathe turned and carved
mahogany combined with
paint and found objects*

DOUGLAS W. JONES AND KIM KULOW-JONES
Jewelry Box, 1999
9"H X 18"W X 13"D (23 X 46 X 33 CM)
Medium-density fiberboard, maple, gold leaf
PHOTOS BY JERRY ANTHONY

**DOUGLAS W. JONES AND
KIM KULOW-JONES**
Eyeglass Shelter with Base, 1996
19"H X 9"W X 7"D (48 X 23 X 18 CM)
Maple, mahogany
PHOTO BY JERRY ANTHONY

*Shaped and pinned maple lid;
shaped mahogany base*

STEVEN CAREAU
Untitled, 2001
6"h x 10"w x 10"d (15 x 25 x 25 cm)
Black walnut, maple burl
PHOTO BY ARTIST

PETRA OHNMACHT

PETRA OHNMACHT
Piggeldi & Frederik, 1998
2¾"H X 2¾"W X 4¾"D
(6 X 6 X 12 CM)
Beech
PHOTO BY MARKUS GELDHAUSER
AND PETRA OHNMACHT

TAMMY SHEFFER-BRACHA
Craft Box, 2002
10¼"H x 24"W x 13⅛"D (26 x 61 x 33 CM)
Walnut, spalted maple
PHOTOS BY BOBBIE BUSH

TAMMY SHEFFER-BRACHA

TAMMY SHEFFER-BRACHA
Box—Alter Style, 2002
8½"H x 7½"W x 7½"D (22 x 19 x 19 CM)
Mahogany, lacewood, metal leaf
PHOTO BY GAIL HANDELMAN

TAMMY SHEFFER-BRACHA

Box—Bier Style, 2002

7"H X 8"W X 6¼"D (18 X 21 X 16 CM)

Mahogany, lacewood, metal leaf

PHOTO BY GAIL HANDELMAN

"By combining aesthetic and utilitarian goals, as well as traditional Western and Oriental elements, I strive to create a contemporary, fresh look."

STEPHEN HATCHER

STEPHEN HATCHER
Surfacing, 2003
3"H x 6"W x 5"D
(8 x 15 x 13 cm)
Cocobolo, stone
PHOTOS BY ARTIST

STEPHEN HATCHER
Seasons of the Orient, 2003
4"H X 8"W X 8"D (10 X 20 X 20 CM)
Macassar ebony, Asian striped ebony
PHOTOS BY ARTIST

DIANE EDWARDS

DIANE EDWARDS
Algonquin Pine, 2002
3½"H X 12"W X 9"D (9 X 31 X 23 CM)
Bird's-eye cherry, gray harewood, big leaf maple,
birch, purpleheart
PHOTO BY KRIS ROSAR

TAM J. CRAWFORD
Untitled, 2002
9"H X 5"W X 5"D
(23 X 13 1X 3 CM).
Padauk, zebrawood
PHOTO BY TERESA POLLEN

Tam J. Crawford
Spider Box, 2002
9"H x 5"W x 5"D
(23 x 13 x 3 cm)
Teak, cocobolo
PHOTO BY TERESA POLLEN

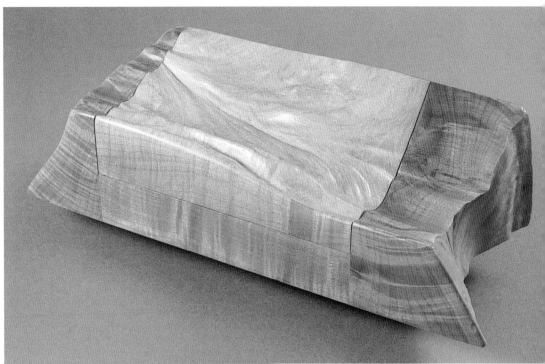

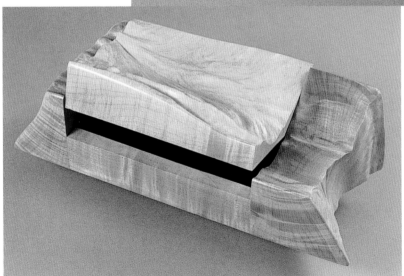

JOHN M. DURUM

JOHN M. DURUM
Barkless Maple Treasure Box, 1999
2½"H x 9"W x 3¾"D (6 x 23 x 10 CM)
Oregon maple
PHOTOS BY ARTIST

JOHN M. DURUM
Wild Cherry Keepsake Box, 2003
3"H X 5½"W X 5½"D (8 X 14 X 14 CM)
Wild cherry, fishtail oak, bloodwood,
purpleheart, Queensland maple, ebony,
Tasmanian myrtle, lacewood, poplar
PHOTO BY ARTIST

JOHN M. DURUM
Large Maple Jewelry Box, 1998
9"H X 14"W X 14"D (23 X 36 X 36 CM)
Oregon maple, Oregon black walnut, wenge, Eastern
fiddleback maple, makore, padauk
PHOTOS BY ARTIST

DONALD DERRY
Spirit Box, 2003
4½"H x 6"W x 6"D (11 x 15 x 15 CM)
Walnut
PHOTOS BY ARTIST

DONALD DERRY
Keepsake Keeper, 2003
8"H X 13½"H X 5"D (20 X 34 X 13 CM)
Black locust, maple burl
PHOTOS BY ARTIST

CHRISTOPHER KUNKLE
Bird's-eye Maple Jewelry Chest, 1999
13"H X 9"W X 6"D (33 X 23 X 15 CM)
Bird's-eye maple
PHOTO BY ARTIST

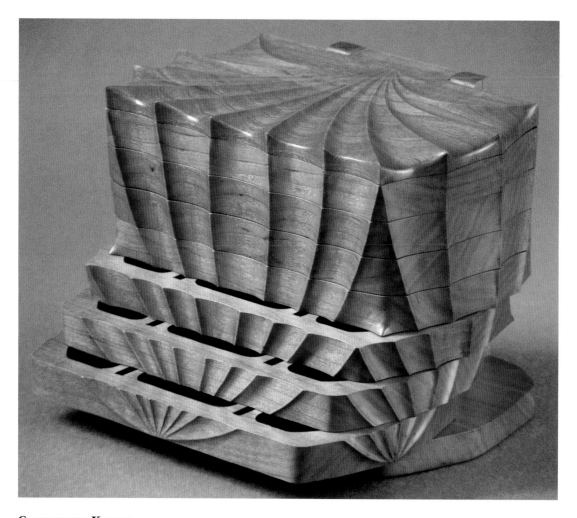

CHRISTOPHER KUNKLE
Cherry Jewelry Chest, 1997
8"H x 11"W x 6"D (20 x 28 x 15 CM)
Cherry
PHOTO BY ARTIST

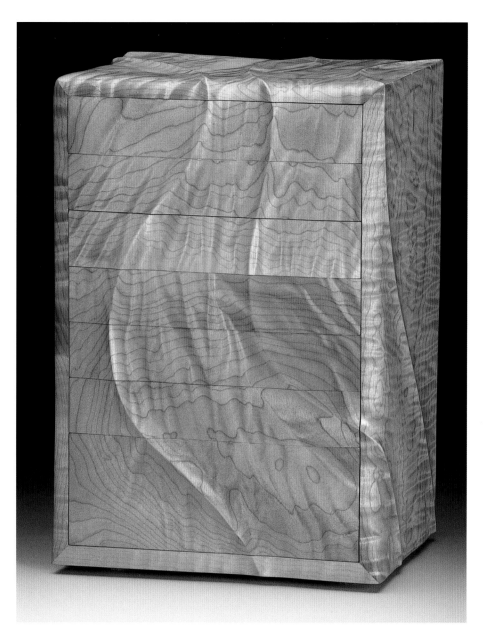

CHRISTOPHER KUNKLE
Icebox, 2001
10"H x 8"W x 6"D
(25 x 20 x 15 CM)
Flame maple
PHOTO BY ARTIST

The drawers open by pushing a button on the back of the box.

MICHAEL JOHN CRAIGDALLIE
Lotus Box, 2002
43"H x 17"W x 17"D (109 x 43 x 43 CM)
Paduak, quilted Western maple, maple
PHOTOS BY ARTIST

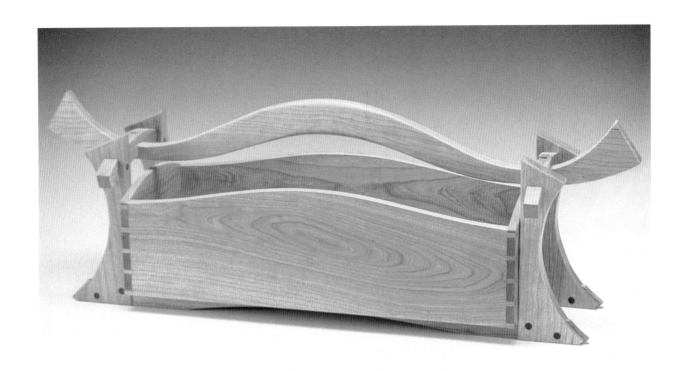

MICHAEL JOHN CRAIGDALLIE
Japanese Styled Tool Box, 2001
8"H X 9"W X 29"D (20 X 23 X 73 CM)
Cherry, walnut
PHOTOS BY ARTIST

MARK TITUS DIEBOLT
Jewelry Armoire, 2003
22"H x 15"W x 9"D
(56 x 38 x 23 CM)
Karelian birch burl, black
walnut, pau ferro
PHOTO BY BRUCE LITOLFF

MARK TITUS DIEBOLT

MARK TITUS DIEBOLT
One-Drawer Jewelry Chest, 2002
9"H X 5"W X 9"D (23 X 13 X 23 CM)
Waterfall bubinga, maple, black obechi
PHOTO BY ARTIST

MARK TITUS DIEBOLT
Jewelry Chest, 2002
6½"H X 15"W X 9"D (17 X 38 X 23 CM)
Quilted sapele, maple, black obechi
PHOTO BY ARTIST

These boxes were hand-veneered.

VICTOR CLAPP

VICTOR CLAPP
Fish, 2003
3"H x 8"W x 5"D (8 x 20 x 13 cm)
Oak, walnut
PHOTO BY STAMBAUGH PHOTOGRAPHIC

VICTOR CLAPP
Butterfly, 2003
3"H x 8"W x 5"D (8 x 20 x 13 cm)
Oak, walnut
PHOTO BY STAMBAUGH PHOTOGRAPHICS

VICTOR CLAPP
Killer Whale, 2003
3"H X 8"W X 5"D
(8 X 20 X 13 CM)
Oak, walnut
PHOTOS BY
STAMBAUGH PHOTOGRAPHICS

BRIAN DONAHUE

BRIAN DONAHUE
Andrea's Treasure (jewelry box), 1996
5½"H x 8"W x 5"D (14 x 20 x 13 CM)
Silver buttonwood
PHOTOS BY ROYAL IMAGES/JAMES KING

Cut from tree stump, band sawed

PETER MALINOSKI
Ice Box, 2002
22"H x 11"W x 11"D (56 x 28 x 28 CM)
Poplar, white ash
PHOTOS BY ARTIST

PETER MALINOSKI
Blue Jewel, 2003
14"H x 17"W x 10"D (36 x 43 x 25 CM)
Poplar, white ash
PHOTO BY ARTIST

JACK ALBERTI
Jericho, 2001
8½"H x 15½"W x 15½"D (22 x 40 x 40 CM)
Swiss pear, mahogany, curly maple, cinnamon laurel burl,
woman's tongue, lemonwood, red oak, holly, felt
PHOTO BY WAYNE DOMBKOWSKI

JACK ALBERTI

The Great Escape and The Greater Escape, 2001
9"H x 8"W x 8"D (23 x 20 x 20 CM) AND
14"H x 7½"W x 7½"D (36 x 19 x 19 CM)

Ebonized cherry, mahogany, Swiss pear, cinnamon laurel burl, woman's tongue, curly maple, lemonwood, red oak, holly, felt

PHOTOS BY WAYNE DOMBKOWSKI

JACK ALBERTI
Ina's Treasure, 1995
8¾"H x 8¾"W x 8¾"D (22 x 22 x 22 CM)
Swiss pear, walnut, holly, 23k gold leaf
PHOTO BY WAYNE DOMBKOWSKI

RANDY COOK

RANDY COOK
Tie Box, 2002
6"H x 9"W x 4"D (15 x 23 x 11 CM)
Holly, ebony, maple, fir, oil finish
PHOTO BY GEORGE POST

RANDY COOK
Sage Box, 2000
9"H x 5"W x 6½"D (23 x 13 x 17 CM)
Holly, ebony, spalted maple
PHOTO BY GEORGE POST

RANDY COOK
Buoy Box, 2000
7"H x 8½"W x 8½"D (18 x 22 x 22 CM)
Rosewood, holly, Western maple
PHOTO BY GEORGE POST

METTE FRUERGAARD-JENSEN
Long Narrow Box, 2000
3½"H x 7¾"W x 1³⁄₁₆"D (9 x 20 x 3 cm)
Wood, aluminum, horn
PHOTO BY ALIKI SAPOUNTZI

METTE FRUERGAARD-JENSEN
Oval Box, 2000
4¼"H x 3½"W x 1⁹⁄₁₆"D
(11 x 9 x 4 CM)
Copper, driftwood, horn
PHOTO BY ALIKI SAPOUNTZI

141

WALLACE W. DREXLER

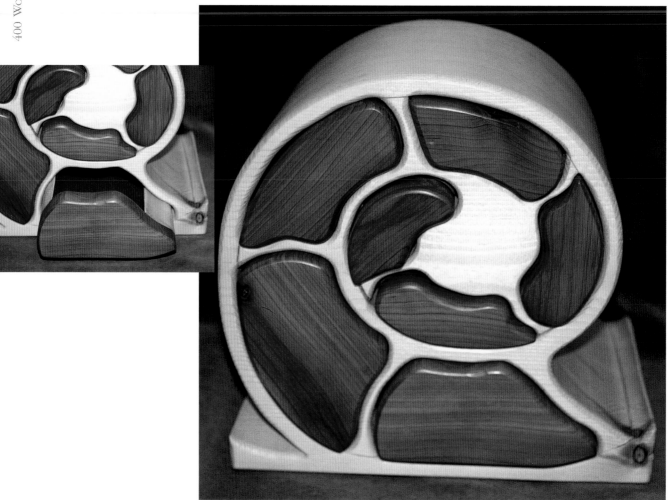

WALLACE W. DREXLER
Cephalopod, 2002
11"H x 11"W x 4½"D (28 x 28 x 11 CM)
Pine, Eastern red cedar
PHOTOS BY ARTIST

WALLACE W. DREXLER
Redwood Burl Highboy, 2002
11"H X 7"W X 4"D
(28 X 18 X 10 CM)
Redwood burl
PHOTO BY ARTIST

TREVOR A. TONEY

TREVOR A. TONEY
Untitled Box, 2003
8"H x 24"W x 9½"D (20 x 61 x 24 CM)
Walnut
PHOTOS BY ARTIST

BOB STREET

Pagoda Jewelry Box, 2003

12½"H x 18"W x 9"D (32 x 46 x 23 CM)

Walnut, curly maple, maple

PHOTO BY MATT BOWMAN

BOB STREET
Tool Chest, 2002
24"H x 14"W x 8"D (61 x 36 x 21 CM)
Walnut, maple, pink ivory wood
PHOTOS BY MATT BOWMAN

PER BRANDSTEDT

PER BRANDSTEDT
Anna Katarina, 1999
8¼"H x 11½"W x 7¾"D (21 x 29 x 20 CM)
Swedish curly birch
PHOTOS BY FRANCIS HOWARD

PER BRANDSTEDT
Jubileum, 2001
7"H X 8"W X 8"D (18 X 20 X 20 CM)
Jacaranda
PHOTO BY FRANCIS HOWARD

PER BRANDSTEDT
Karl Gustav, 1997
7"H X 10½"W X 7½"D (18 X 27 X 19 CM)
Swedish curly birch, plastic
PHOTO BY FRANCIS HOWARD

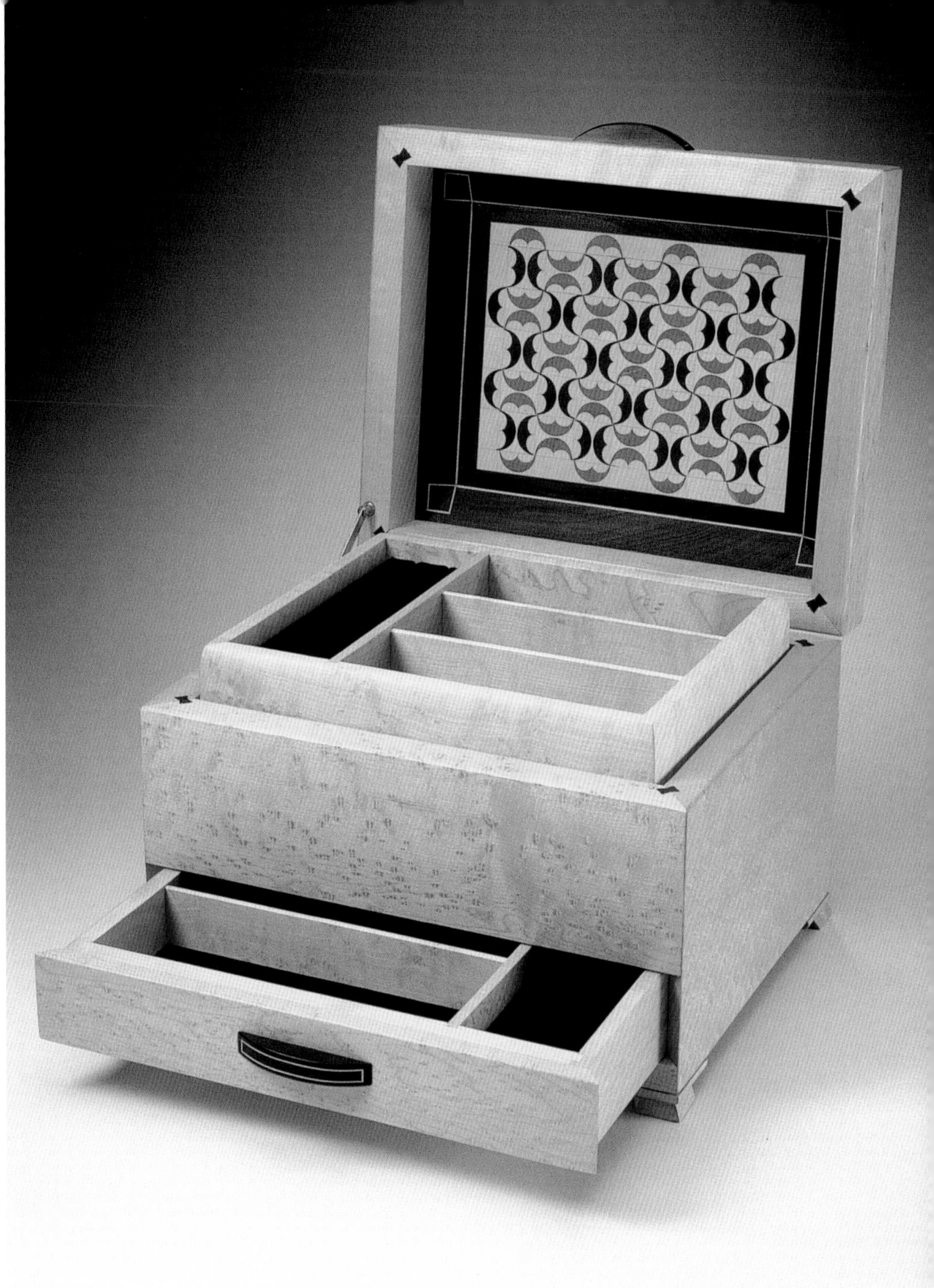

AL LADD
*Running Delta
Jewelry Box,* 1997
8"H X 11"W X 6"D
(20 X 28 X 15 CM)
Holly, cherry, Peruvian walnut,
bird's-eye maple, ebony

PHOTO BY JONATHAN WALLEN

149

AL LADD

Dalbergia Garden Jewelry Box, 1998

8"H X 12"W X 8"D (20 X 31 X 20 CM)

Brazilian tulipwood, holly, walnut, curly maple, honey locust, macassar ebony, curly cherry

PHOTO BY JONATHAN WALLEN

AL LADD

Arts + Crafts Style Jewelry Box, 1998

8"H x 11"W x 7"D (20 x 28 x 18 CM)

Spalted maple, jatoba, wenge, leopard wood, ebony

PHOTO BY JONATHAN WALLEN

SCOTT PLACE
Bracelet Box, 2003
5½"H x 5"w x 5"D
(14 x 13 x 13 CM)
Oak, glazed porcelain,
copper
PHOTO BY ARTIST

RANDY MILLER
Crown Box, 2002
5"H X 10"W X 7"D
(13 X 25 X 18 CM)
Curly maple, ebony
PHOTO BY ARTIST

RANDY MILLER
Crown Box, 2002
5"H X 10"W X 6½"D
(13 X 25 X 17 CM)
Pear, blistered maple
PHOTO BY ARTIST

RANDY MILLER
3 Drawer Jewelry Box, 2002
10"H x 14"W x 8"D (25 x 36 x 20 CM)
Curly maple, ebony
PHOTO BY BERNARD WOLF

RAY GARY
The Treasure Box, 2002
2½"H x 12"w x 7"D (6 x 31 x 18 cm)
Cocobolo, canary wood
PHOTO BY KEN KOLLEGE, FAIRBANKS, ALASKA

RAY GARY
Denali Flow, 2002
9"H x 16"W x 8"D (23 x 41 x 20 CM)
Myrtle, cocobolo
PHOTO BY KEN KOLLEGE, FAIRBANKS, ALASKA

RAY GARY
The Empire Box, 2002
4"H x 4"W x 7"D (10 x 10 x 18 CM)
Narra, mesquite
PHOTO BY KEN KOLLEGE, FAIRBANKS, ALASKA

ROGER HEITZMAN

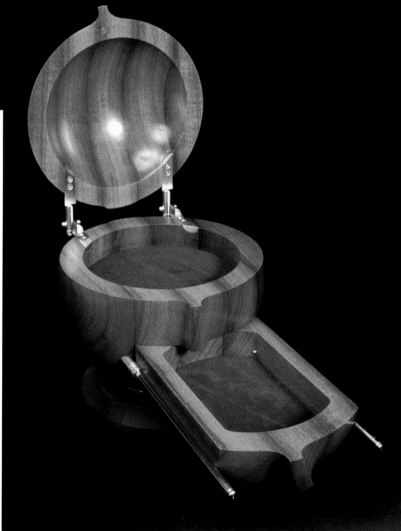

ROGER HEITZMAN
Cosmo, 2001
8½" (22 CM) SPHERE
Wood
PHOTOS BY ARTIST

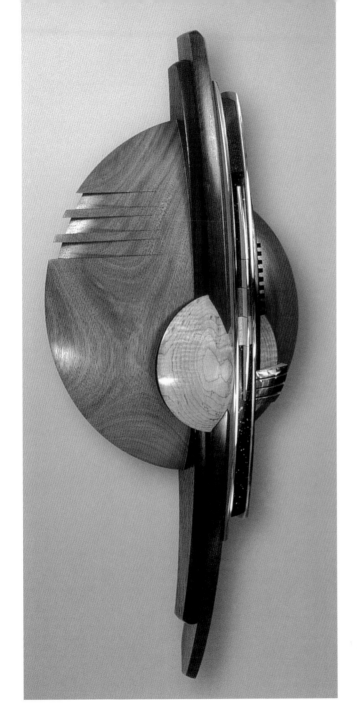

ROGER HEITZMAN
Perihelion, 2001
45"H x 19"W x 9"D (114 x 49 x 23 CM)
Wood, aluminum, resin-based granite
PHOTOS BY ARTIST

ROGER GIFKINS
Small Treasure, 2001
2¼"H x 4¾"W x 4¾"D (6 x 12 x 12 CM)
Rosewood, satinwood, mangrove, bamboo
PHOTO BY ARTIST

ROGER GIFKINS
Oriental Box, 2001
3½"H x 9"w x 4"D (9 x 23 x 10 cm)
Satinwood
PHOTOS BY ARTIST

These boxes were inspired by an 11th century sushi press and feature Japanese double end grain joints on the trays.

ROGER GIFKINS
Oriental Box, 2001
3½"H x 9"w x 4"D
(9 x 23 x 10 cm)
Ebony
PHOTO BY ARTIST

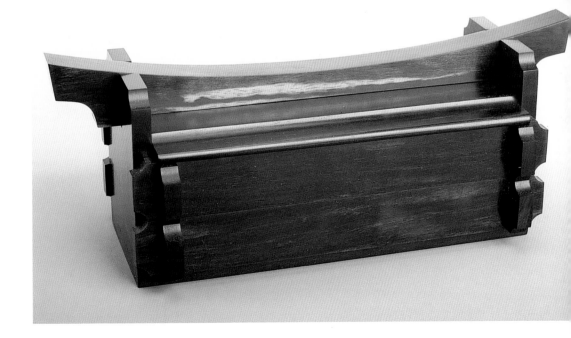

ROGER GIFKINS
Jewelry Box, 2001
5½"H x 12½"W x 9"D (14 x 32 x 23 cm)
Rosewood, gidgee, silver ash, ebony
PHOTO BY WARREN CROZIER

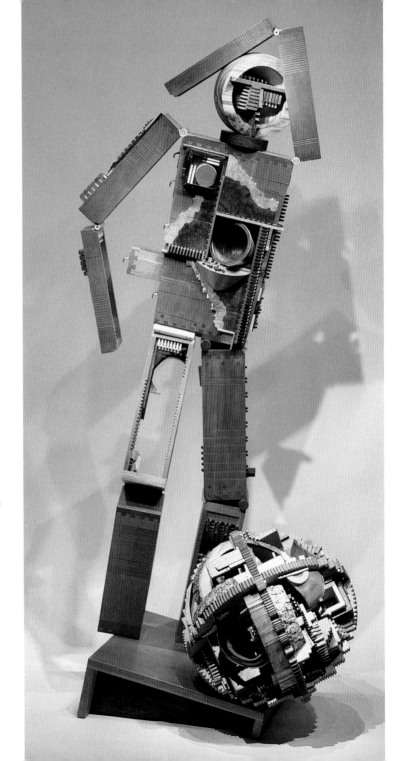

PO SHUN LEONG
Football, 2002
60"H X 41"W X 16"D (152 X 104 X 41 CM)
Mahogany
PHOTO BY ARTIST

This box features various wood, wood turnings, historic woods, compartments in arms and legs, and a revolving head.

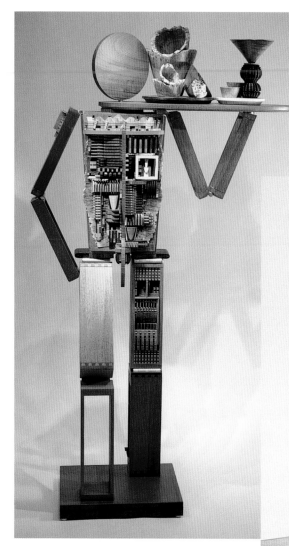

PO SHUN LEONG
Butler, 2002
60"H X 36"W X 13"D (152 X 92 X 33 CM)
Mahogany
PHOTOS BY ARTIST

PO SHUN LEONG

Ark, 2003
76"H X 53"W X 11"D
(193 X 135 X 28 CM)

Cherry burl, koa, mahogany, maple, wenge, ebony, purleheart, pink ivory, buckeye burl, pernambuco, palm, zebrawood, pau Amarillo

PHOTOS BY ARTIST

Po Shun Leong

Tower Box, 2000

72"H X 12"W X 11"D (183 X 31 X 28 CM)

Mahogany, maple, wenge, ebony, cherry burl, lighting

PHOTOS BY ARTIST

Tower Box features crystal glass cubes by artist Latchezar Boyadijev

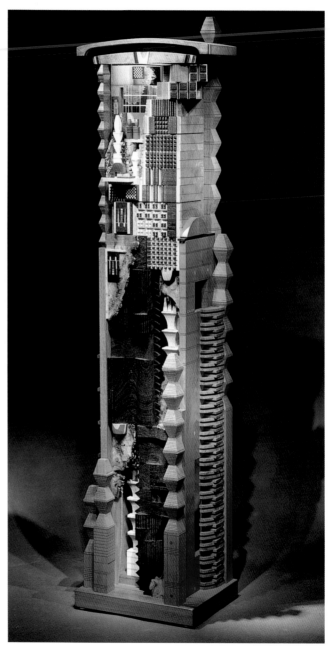

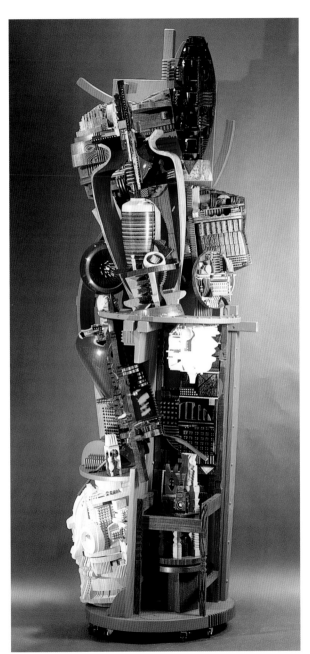

PO SHUN LEONG
Hell Box, 2001
91"H x 26"W x 26"D (231 x 66 x 66 CM)
Various woods
PHOTOS BY ARTIST

BRUCE SHAW

BRUCE SHAW
Jewelry Box #1, 2002
15"H x 9"W x 11"D
(38 x 23 x 28 CM)
Brazilian rosewood
PHOTO BY CHRIS GAGE

JIM LEITER
Curly Maple/Ebony Three Drawer Box, 2000
8"H x 15"W x 7"D (21 x 38 x 18 CM)
Curly maple, ebony
PHOTO BY MATT MEADOWS

JIM LEITER
*Curly Cherry, Macassar
Ebony Box,* 2002
6"H X 13"W X 8"D
(15 X 33 X 20.5 CM)
Curly cherry, Macassar
ebony, brass
PHOTO BY NATHAN SIMONIS

*The lid sides are shaped to
hold a drawer to allow full
view of contents.*

JIM LEITER
*Australian Blackwood
Box,* 2002
3"H X 9"W X 6"D
(8 X 23 X 15 CM)
Austrailian blackwood,
rosewood, brass
PHOTO BY NATHAN SIMONIS

MICHAEL J. BROLLY
www.jewel@space.re:, 1998
Mahogany, maple, purple-
heart, bubinga, ebony, brass,
gold leaf

PHOTOS BY DAVID HAAS

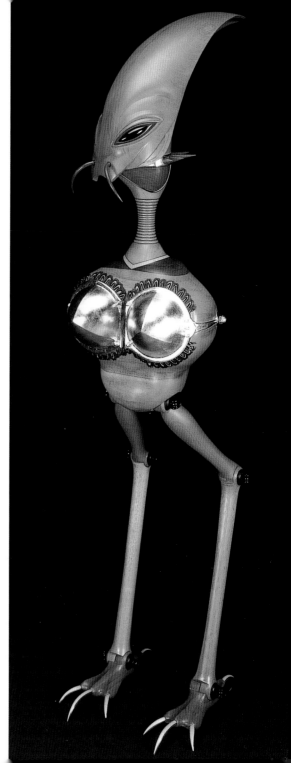

*Collection of
Fleur Breesler*

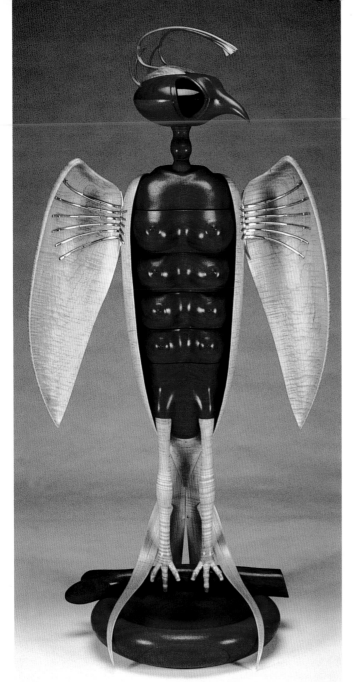

MICHAEL J. BROLLY
Thinking of My Mother-in-Law Marianne and Those Magnificent Mahogany Breasts (jewelry box), 1996
Mahogany, maple, walnut, ebony, brass, magnets
PHOTOS BY DAVID HAAS

Collection of Rose Carney

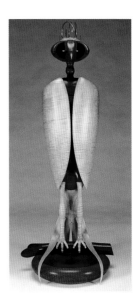

MICHAEL J. BROLLY
Io: A Turned Box, 2001
2"H X 2"W (5 X 5 CM)
Maple, mahogany, gold leaf
PHOTOS BY MITCH MANDEL

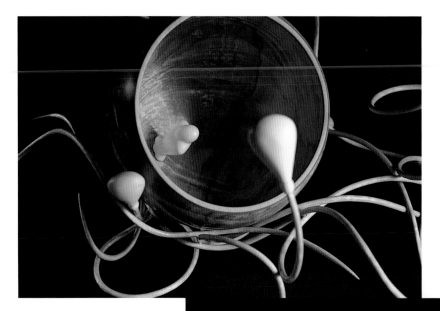

Collection of Fleur Breesler

MICHAEL J. BROLLY
*Self Portrait of the Artist as a
Very, Very Young Man,* 1997
14"H X 22"W X 12"D
(36 X 56 X 31 CM)
Maple, holly, cherry
PHOTOS BY ARTIST

JOHN WIGGERS
Gaia Jewelry Chest, 1999
12 3/8"H x 7 1/8"W x 7 1/8"D (31 x 18 x 18 CM)
Curly Moave, mahogany, sapele
PHOTO BY JOHN GLOS

*This box features a dadoed curly Moave panel,
mahogany quarter round corners, sapele drawer
fronts, and dovetail joinery.*

BLAISE GASTON

BLAISE GASTON
Jewelry Box, 1996
16"H X 14"W X 18"D (41 X 36 X 46 CM)
Cherry, fishtail oak
PHOTO BY PHILIP BEAURLINE

LEW LAMBERT
Untitled, 2002
18"H x 24"W x 12"D
(46 x 61 x 31 CM)
Black walnut, crotch
walnut, curly maple
PHOTOS BY VINCENT MCDONALD

LEW LAMBERT
Pink Bombé, 2002
3½"H x 11"W x 11"D
(9 x 28 x 28 CM)
Bird's-eye maple, pink ivory
PHOTO BY VINCENT MCDONALD

LEW LAMBERT
Untitled, 2003
2"H x 8"W x 3¾"D (5 x 20 x 9 CM)
Tulip, quilted maple, pink ivory,
ebony
PHOTO BY VINCENT MCDONALD

LEW LAMBERT
Untitled, 2002
9½"H x 15"W x 12"D
(26 x 38 x 31 CM)
Black walnut, spalted
maple
PHOTOS BY VINCENT MCDONALD

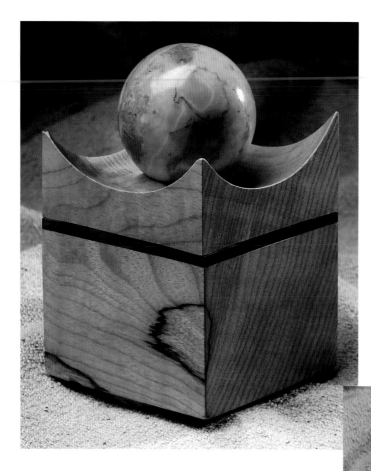

LEN MAZZOCCO
Marble Box, 2002
5"H X 3"W X 3"D (13 X 8 X 8 CM)
Chestnut, cocobolo, marble
PHOTOS BY MIKE LEVASHAFF

LEN MAZZOCCO
Untitled, 2002
5"H x 3"W x 3"D (31 x 8 x 8 CM)
Chestnut, cocobolo, walnut
PHOTOS BY MIKE LEVASHAFF

LEN MAZZOCCO
Maple, Walnut Bud Box, 2003
12"H x 3"W x 3"D (31 x 8 x 8 CM)
Burl maple, walnut
PHOTO BY MIKE LEVASHAFF

*This box's top separates from its
bottom to reveal a secret storage area.*

THOMAS R. IRVEN
Eggcorn, 2001
3½"H x 8½"W x 3½"D (9 x 22 x 9 CM)
Cocobolo, bird's-eye maple
PHOTO BY ARTIST

THOMAS R. IRVEN
Acorn Box, 1999
2¼"H x 5"w x 2¼"D (6 x 13 x 6 cm)
Wormy pear, walnut
PHOTO BY ARTIST

"My designs come from nature, dreams, and life experiences. I strive to create forms that are creative, playful, and able to stand the test of time."

R. THOMAS TEDROWE, JR
Alex's Box, 1996
11½"H X 7"W X 7"D (30 X 18 X 18 CM)
Macassar ebony, curly maple
PHOTO BY ARTIST

This box was inspired by Oriental stacking lunch boxes.

R. THOMAS TEDROW, JR
Mikoshigura, 1990
8"H X 12"W X 12"D (20 X 31 X 31 CM).
Bubinga, cherry, cedar
PHOTO BY ARTIST

This box is the artist's version of a miniature Japanese traditional storehouse.

R. THOMAS TEDROW, JR
Turned Hickory Box, 1978
12"H X 7"W (31 X 18 CM).
Hickory
PHOTOS BY STEVE MANN

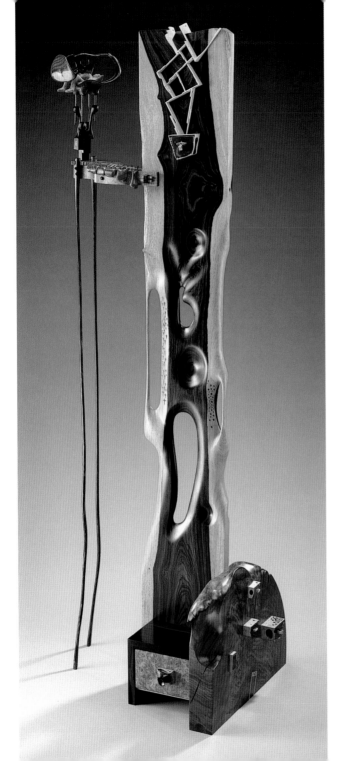

CHRISTOPHER W. CANTWELL
Walk, 2002
61"H x 21"W x 17"D (155 x 53 x 43 CM)
Exotic woods
PHOTOS BY HAP SAKWA

CHRISTOPHER W. CANTWELL
Trinity, 2001
18"H x 15"W x 4"D
(46 x 38 x 10 CM)
Exotic woods
PHOTOS BY GEORGE POST

CHRISTOPHER W. CANTWELL
Wonderland, 1996
12"H x 8"W x 4"D
(31 x 20 x 10 CM)
Exotic woods
PHOTO BY GEORGE POST

*"I work with the wood and my own
ideas when I make my designs.
Often, the challenge of using a
grain pattern in the best way, or
working with a particular piece of
wood, will inspire me."*

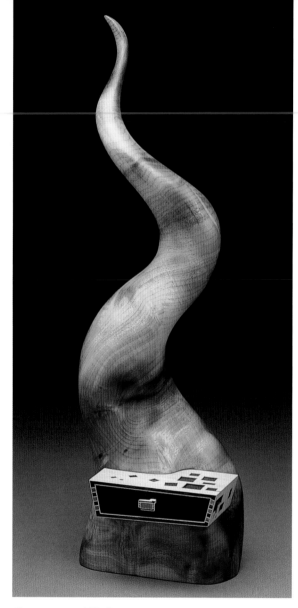

CHRISTOPHER W. CANTWELL
Ghost Box, 1998
17"H X 6"W X 4"D (43 X 15 X 10 CM)
Bay laurel, ebony, exotic woods
PHOTO BY GEORGE POST

CHRISTOPHER W. CANTWELL
Clouds (Left) and Dark and Wiggly (Right)
EACH APPROX. 65"H X 14"W X 10"D (165 X 36 X 25 CM)
Tulip, ziricote, exotic woods
PHOTO BY GEORGE POST

Tall Wiggly series boxes wiggle when a drawer is opened.

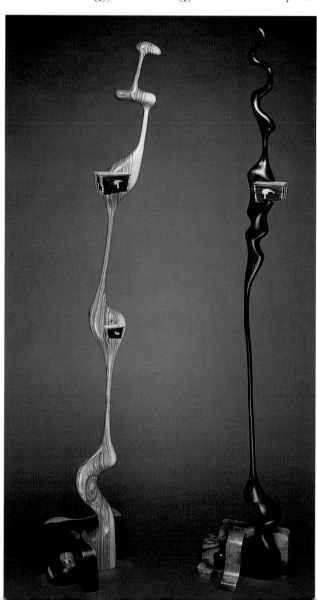

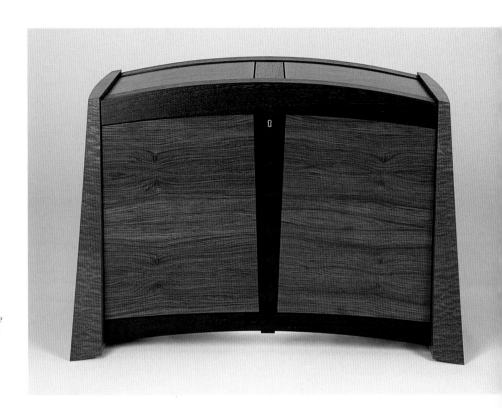

"One of two identical trunks. This one is for my wife and son. The other was made for friends, in memory of their late son, Braxton."

THOMAS J. MONAHAN

THOMAS J. MONAHAN
Words Unspoken, 2002
24"H X 36¾"W X 22"D (61 X 93 X 56 CM)
Cocobolo, pommele sapele, wenge, cherry, maple
PHOTOS BY LON MONAHAN

STEVEN KOSTER

STEVEN KOSTER
Mantaba, 2002
9½"H x 8½"W (24 x 22 CM)
Basswood
PHOTO BY JUN KWON

*Courtesy of Kendall College
of Art and Design*

SCOTT NAYLOR

SCOTT NAYLOR
Relationships, 2002
9"H x 12"W x 9"D (23 x 31 x 23 CM)
Basswood, plexiglass
PHOTO BY JUN KWON

Courtesy of Kendall College of Art and Design

MATTHIAS PLIESSNIG
Vessel, 2002
6½"H x 6½"W x 35"D
(17 x 17 x 89 CM)
Walnut, steel
PHOTOS BY MARK JOHNSON

YANG JUN KWON
*The Boy Came From
California II,* 2002
6"H X 8"W X 6"D
(15 X 21 X 15 CM)
Basswood, gold leaf,
brass, broom
PHOTO BY ARTIST

YANG JUN KWON

YANG JUN KWON
The Boy Came From California I, 2002
6"H X 11"W X 4½"D (15 X 28 X 12 CM)
Basswood, gold leaf, brass, broom
PHOTOS BY ARTIST

MARTINE CONVISER
Bead Box, 2002
8"H x 8"W x 8"D (20 x 20 x 20 CM)
Mahogany, silver, suede
PHOTOS BY ARTIST

MARTINE CONVISER
Sphere Boxes, 2001
LARGE: 4" DIAMETER (10 CM); SMALL: 3½" DIAMETER (9 CM)
Maple, pau ferra, paper
PHOTOS BY ARTIST

GLYNN SHEPPARD
Walnut Box with Interlocking Lid, 2003
1 ¾"H X 3"W X 1 ¾"D (5 X 8 X 5 CM)
Walnut, exotic woods
PHOTO BY ARTIST

GLYNN SHEPPARD
Single Ring Pyramid Box, 2001
3"H X 4"W X 4"D (8 X 10 X 10 CM)
Sycamore, African blackwood
PHOTOS BY ARTIST

MICHAEL GREGORY

MICHAEL GREGORY
Rose Box, 1999
4"H x 8"W x 4"D (11 x 20 x 11 cm)
Rosewood, silver ash
PHOTOS BY ARTIST

MICHAEL GREGORY
Small Box, 2000
4"H x 7"W x 4"D (9 x 17 x 10 CM)
Rosewood, silver ash, silky oak, ebony

SETH MARTIN PEGMAN

SETH MARTIN PEGMAN
Crutch, 2002
10"H x 12"W x 8"D (26 x 31 x 20 CM)
Basswood
PHOTO BY JUN KWON

*Courtesy of Kendall College of
Art and Design*

MARK SFIRRI

MARK SFIRRI
Mini Truffle Chest, 2002
5¼"H x 9½"W x 7"D (13 x 24 CM)
Mahogany, gold leaf
PHOTOS BY ARTIST

*Courtesy of Kendall
College of Art and Design*

JEREMY COX
Solitude, 2001
17"H X 23"W X 6"D (43 X 58 X 15 CM)
Basswood, found materials
PHOTOS BY JUN KWON

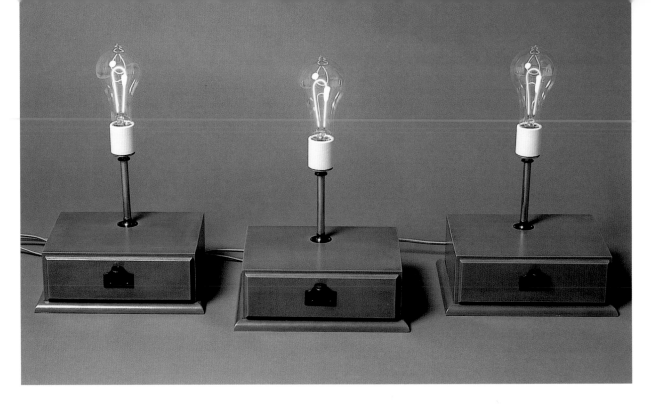

KATIE SANNER
Words To Go By, 1998
15"H x 10"W x 7½"D (38 x 25 x 19 CM)
Maple, paper, metal, light bulbs
PHOTOS BY MICHAEL JAMES

GLENN ELVIG
Pointy, 2003
20"H X 12"W X 8"D
(51 X 31 X 20 CM)
Tupelo, pencils, sharpener
PHOTO BY ARTIST

*This box represents the
letter P in the artist's
alphabet teabox series.*

GLENN ELVIG
Manatee, 2001
12"H X 12"W X 12"D
(31 X 31 X 31 CM)
Maple burl, dolls
PHOTO BY ARTIST

This box represents the letter M in the artist's alphabet teabox series.

GLENN ELVIG
On the QT, 2003
13"H X 22"W X 14"D (33 X 56 X 36 CM)
Tupelo, pool cue, billiard balls
PHOTO BY ARTIST

*This box represents the letter Q in
the artist's alphabet teabox series.*

GLENN ELVIG
Realty, 2000
10"H X 5"W X 5"D (26 X 13 X 13CM)
Myrtle burl, fishing reel
PHOTO BY ARTIST

*This box represents the letter R in the
artist's alphabet teabox series.*

205

GLENN ELVIG
Perpendicularity, 2003
8"H x 16"W x 8"D (20 x 41 x 20 CM)
Figured myrtle, metal
PHOTO BY ARTIST

ROBERT INGHAM
Small Treasure Boxes, 2001
1"H X 5"W X 5'D (3 X 12 X 12 CM)
Various woods, patinated copper pivot caps
PHOTO BY ARTIST

The boxes feature sprung pivoting lids.

ROBERT INGHAM
Quatrefoil, 1999
2¾"H x 8"H x 8"W (7 x 20 x 20 CM)
Pear, king wood
PHOTO BY ARTIST

Spring loaded pivots counter shrinkage.

ROBERT INGHAM,
*Elaine's Treasure
Chest,* 2000.
10"H x 17"W x 8"D
(25 x 43 x 20 CM)
Black walnut burr,
ripple sycamore, brass
PHOTO BY ARTIST

Side drawers pivot.

ROBERT INGHAM
Trio, 2002
6"H x 18"W x 6"D (15 x 45 x 15 CM)
Four-thousand-year-old bog oak, masur birch,
olive ash, boxwood
PHOTO BY ARTIST

ROBERT INGHAM
Duet, 2002
2"H X 13¾"W X 7¼"D (5 X 35 X 18 CM)
Walnut, masur birch, lacewood
PHOTO BY ARTIST

GEOFFREY G. CARSON
25th Anniversary Jewelry Box, 2003
24"H X 18"W X 7½"D (61 X 46 X 19 CM)
Pennsylvania gum cherry, velvet, virgin Pennsylvania cherry,
bird's-eye maple, sycamore, Port Orford cedar, ironwood
PHOTOS BY ERIC FOX

DAVID FOBES

DAVID FOBES
Hex 3, 2002
22"DIA. (56 CM)
Birch, eucalyptus, red gum
PHOTO BY ARTIST

DAVID FOBES
Hex 1, 2002
22"DIA. (56 CM)
Birch, mulberry
PHOTO BY ARTIST

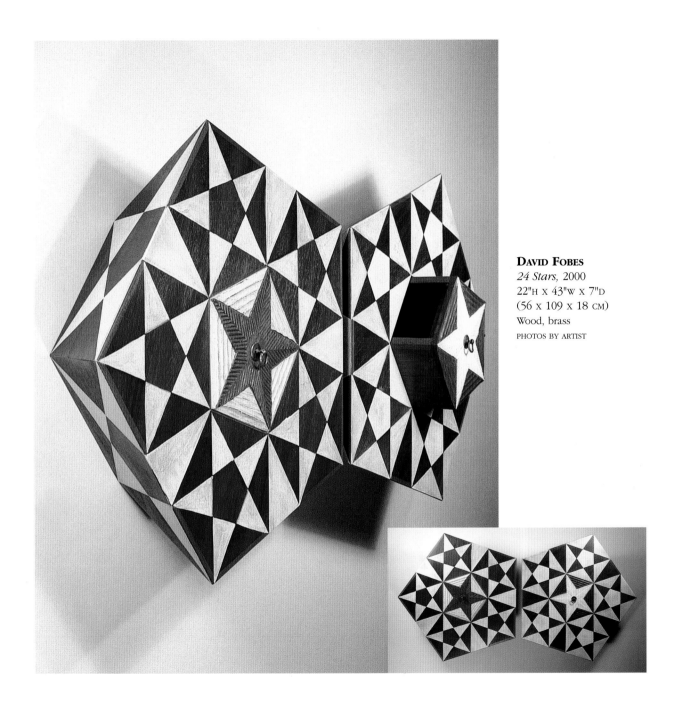

DAVID FOBES
24 Stars, 2000
22"H X 43"W X 7"D
(56 X 109 X 18 CM)
Wood, brass
PHOTOS BY ARTIST

213

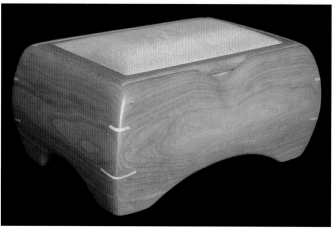

EMILY PALM
Sculpted Cherry and Birdseye Maple Box, 2002
5½"H x 12"w x 9"D (14 x 31 x 23 CM)
Cherry, bird's-eye maple
PHOTOS BY ARTIST

EMILY PALM
*Curly Maple and Spalted
Koa Jewelry Box,* 2002
3½"H x 10"W x 7"H
(9 x 25 x 18 CM)
Curly maple, spalted koa
PHOTOS BY ARTIST

JOHN C. LEE
Idaho Mountain Mahogany
Folding Box, 2001
2½"H x 5"W x 2½"D (6 x 13 x 6 CM)
Mahogany
PHOTOS BY ARTIST

JOHN C. LEE

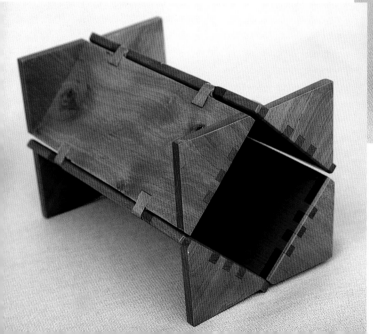

This box was turned inside out, half open.

This box was turned inside out.

JOHN C. LEE
Folding Box, 1999
1¾"H X 3¼"W X 1¾"D (4 X 8 X 4 CM)
Spalted maple, ebony, bloodwood
PHOTOS BY ARTIST

The design is not inlaid, but instead goes through the sides. This box was turned inside out.

THOMAS CABEZAS
Sunrise Jewelry Box, 2002
8"H x 13"W x 8"D (20 x 33 x 20 CM)
Lacewood, padauk, wenge, maple
PHOTO BY BILL LEMKE

THOMAS CABEZAS
Temple Jewelry Box, 2002
8"H x 13"W x 8"D (21 x 33 x 21 CM)
Curly maple, bubinga, wenge, mahogany, bocote
PHOTO BY BILL LEMKE

BRIAN M. CONDRAN

BRIAN M. CONDRAN
Beauty Within, 1996
18½"H x 11½"W x 10½"D (47 x 30 x 27 CM)
Quilted maple, various woods
PHOTOS BY SETH JANOFSKY

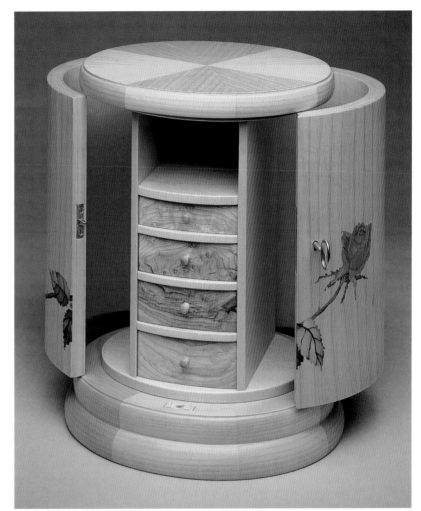

BRIAN M. CONDRAN
Rose Case, 2000
10"H X 8"W X 7"D (26 X 20 X 18 CM)
Mendocino cypress, pink ivory wood, blood wood, poplar, lignum

PHOTOS BY KATHLEEN BELLESILES

JAY ROGERS
Draped Jewelry Box, 1999
6"H x 11"W x 6"D (15 x 28 x 15 CM)
Cherry, costello, bird's-eye maple
PHOTO BY SCOTT CHASTEEN

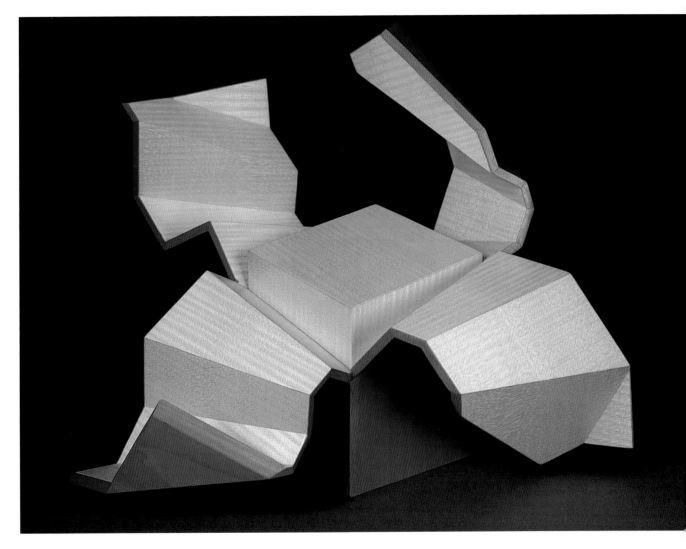

JAY ROGERS
Beginning Again, 2002
14"H x 11"W x 10"D (36 x 28 x 25 CM)
Pear, English sycamore
PHOTO BY JEFF MAGIDSON

JAY ROGERS
Opened Jewelry Box, 1999
6"H X 9"W X 8"D (15 X 23 X 20 CM)
Sapele, satinwood, mahogany
PHOTOS BY SCOTT CHASTEEN

JAY ROGERS
Flame, 2001
13"H x 5"W x 5"D (33 x 13 x 13 CM)
Bloodwood, satinwood, figured makore
PHOTO BY JEFF MAGIDSON

*The inner pink-colored part of the flame
is a lid. It lifts off the hexagonal container
wrapped inside the flame.*

JAY ROGERS
Gyre, 2000
15"H x 6"W x 5"D (38 x 15 x 13 CM)
Andiroba, madrone burl, curly maple
PHOTO BY SCOTT CHASTEEN

*The top section of the bent box shape lifts off to
reveal a mahogany sleeve, which is a container.
This lifts out to expose the rest of the box.*

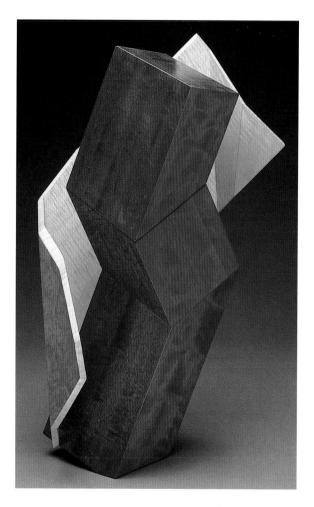

225

MICHAEL HOSALUK
Family, 1999
18"H x 12"W x 8"D
(46 x 31 x 20 CM)
Maple
PHOTOS BY GRANT KERNAN/AK PHOTOS

ADRIAN FRENCH

Message Container 7, A Constructed Conversation, 2002
13½"H x 7"w x 7"D (33 x 18 x 18 cm)

Various woods, ceramic

PHOTOS BY ARTIST

This work is part of a series of long distance collaborations titled Constructed Conversations.

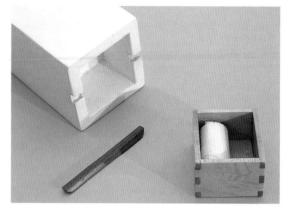

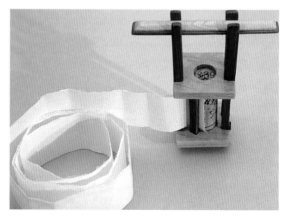

ADRIAN FRENCH
Message Container 4, A Constructed Conversation, 2002
6"H x 2¼"W x 2¼"D (15 x 6 x 6 CM)
Cedar, maple, cork, rice paper
PHOTOS BY ARTIST

ADRIAN FRENCH, FELICIA SZORAD, TRAVIS TOWNSEND
MC 1, A Constructed Conversation, 2001-2003
5"H x 10"W x 5"D (13 x 25 x 13 CM)
Cedar, mixed metals, rice paper
PHOTOS BY ARTISTS

TINA CHINN
Optimo, 2001
2"H x 13"W x 10"D (5 x 33 x 26 CM)
Mahogany, found cigar box, color copy
PHOTOS BY KIM HARRINGTON

TINA CHINN

*"I am constantly on the hunt for found objects
that allow me to get away with as little
woodworking as possible."*

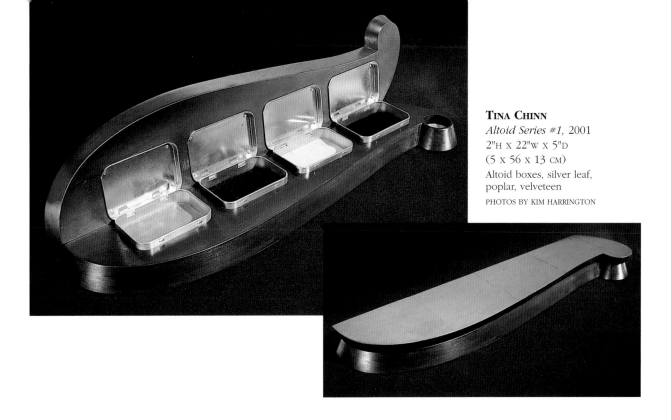

TINA CHINN
Altoid Series #1, 2001
2"H X 22"W X 5"D
(5 X 56 X 13 CM)
Altoid boxes, silver leaf,
poplar, velveteen
PHOTOS BY KIM HARRINGTON

TINA CHINN
Altoid Series—Cane, 2002
2"H X 22"W X 5"D
(5 X 56 X 13 CM)
Altoid boxes, glass cane,
poplar, velveteen
PHOTOS BY ALBERT LAU

WILLIAM McDOWELL

WILLIAM McDOWELL
Drop Front Ring Box, 2002
3½"H X 3½"W X 8"D (9 X 9 X 21 CM)
Hardwoods
PHOTO BY WILLIAM GANDINO

WILLIAM McDOWELL
Jewelry Box, 2003
8"H x 11"W x 5"D
(21 x x28 x 13 CM)
Hardwoods
PHOTO BY WILLIAM GANDINO

WILLIAM McDOWELL
Tekno Jewelry Box, 2003
6"H x 12"W x 8"D
(15.2 x 31 x 20.3 CM)
Black walnut, mahogany,
wenge, curly maple
PHOTO BY ARTIST

ANGUS ROSS

ANGUS ROSS
Earring Cabinet, 1999
15½"H x 10¼"W x 7¾"D
(39.5 x 26 x 20 CM)
Maple, American walnut, leather
PHOTOS BY ARTIST

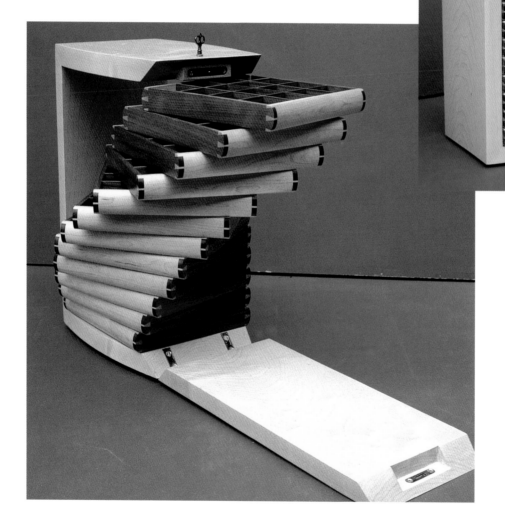

ANGUS ROSS
Medicine Cabinet, 1994
15"H x 9½"W x 6"D (38 x 24 x 15 CM)
Burr ash, English walnut
PHOTOS BY BENEDICT CAMPBELL

DAVID W. SCOTT

Flying Saucer Box, Rocket Ship Boxes, 2003

LARGE: 12"H X 11"DIA. (30 X 28 CM)
Madrone burl, maple

MEDIUM: 9"H X 12"DIA. (23 X 30 CM)
Purpleheart, wormy maple

SMALL: 4"H X 6"DIA. (10 X 15 CM)
Wenge, maple

PHOTO BY TIM BARNWELL

DAVID W. SCOTT

ANDREW POTOCNIK
Floating Box, 1991
4¾"H x 7¾"W x 3½"D (12 x 20 x 9 CM)
Peruvian walnut, silver ash
PHOTO BY ROBERT COLVIN

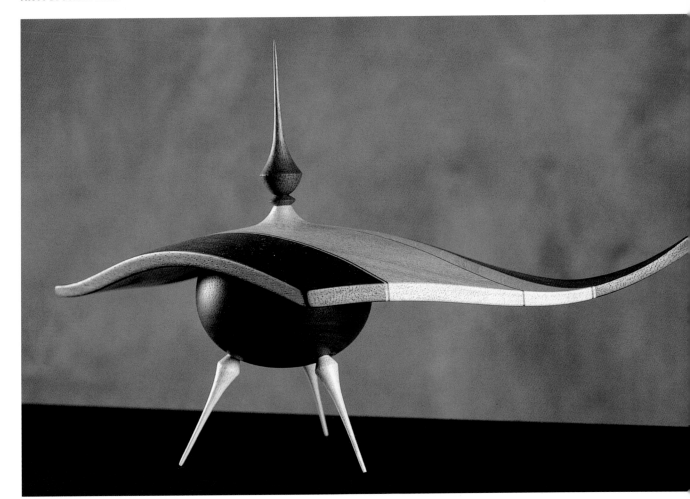

ANDREW POTOCNIK
Surya Box I, 1996
2¾"H x 7"DIAM. (6 x 18 CM)
Xanthorrea, huon pine, date palm
PHOTOS BY NEIL THOMPSON

Collection of Ron and Anita Wornick

ANDREW POTOCNIK
Rocket Boxes, 1998
7¾"H X 3½"DIAM. (20 X 9 CM)
Red gum, aluminum
PHOTO BY NEIL THOMPSON

ANDREW POTOCNIK
Emperor Boxes, 2000
4¼"H X 1¾"DIAM. (11 X 4.5 CM)
Canthium, sandalwood, spinifex acacia
PHOTO BY ARTIST

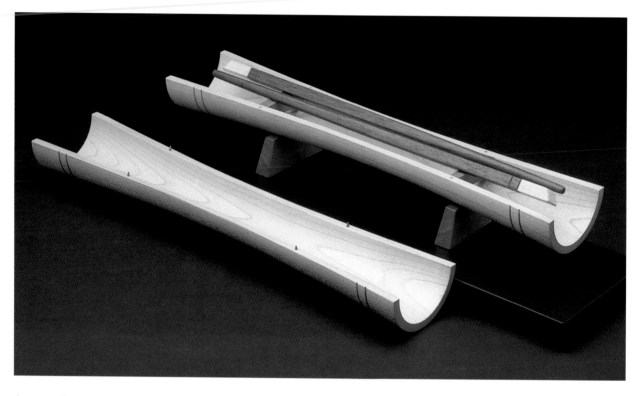

ANDREW POTOCNIK
Chopsticks Box, 1997
2½"H x 10½"w x 2¼"D (6.5 x 27 x 5.5 CM)
Rock maple, red gum
PHOTO BY NEIL THOMPSON

Collection of Texas State Bank

MARTIN LANE

MARTIN LANE
Celebration Humidor, 1999
21¼"H x 25"W x 13¼"D
(54 x 64.5 x 34 CM)
Bubinga, kevasingo, ebony, cedar, rippled
sycamore, sterling silver, silver plate, glass,
silk, glass beads, suede

PHOTOS BY BLANTERN & DAVIS

MARTIN LANE
Chest of Drawers, 1996
18¾"H x 11¾"W x 11¾"D (48 x 30 x 30 cm)
Wenge, burr yew, Honduras cedar
PHOTOS BY BLANTERN & DAVIS

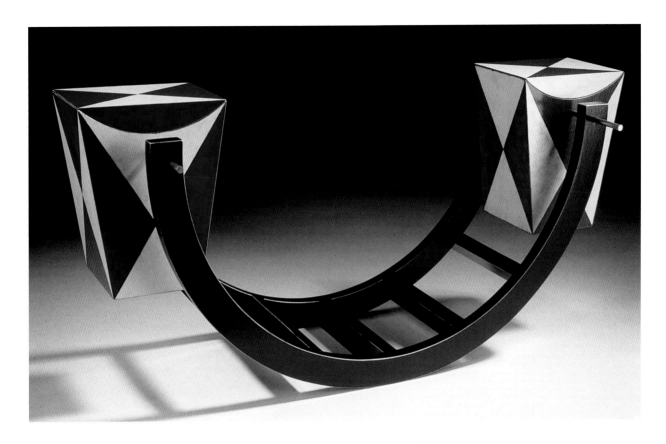

EMI OZAWA

EMI OZAWA
Seesaw 2, 2001
9"H X 19½"W X 8"D (23 X 50 X 21 CM)
Apple plywood, maple, brass
PHOTOS BY MARK JOHNSTON

This box moves like a seesaw when a lid is lifted.

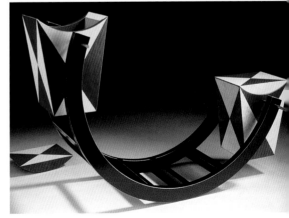

EMI OZAWA
Quack-Quack, 1999
13"H x 17"W x 15"D (33 x 43 x 38 CM)
Apple plywood, cherry
PHOTO BY MARK JOHNSTON

*The lid (duck mouth) opens as you pull the
blue box or turn the orange disc.*

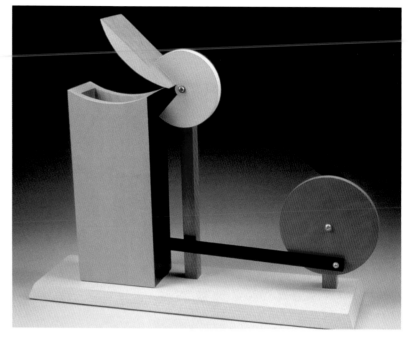

EMI OZAWA
Limes and Oranges, 1996
7"H x 20"W x 2¼"D
(18 x 51 x 6 CM)
Poplar
PHOTO BY DEAN POWELL

*The blocks serve as lids and
for enjoyment.*

Emi Ozawa

Pendulum Box, 1999

9½"H x 4½"W x 5½"D (24 x 12 x 14 CM)

Poplar, brass

PHOTOS BY MARK JOHNSTON

The lid swings like a pendulum.

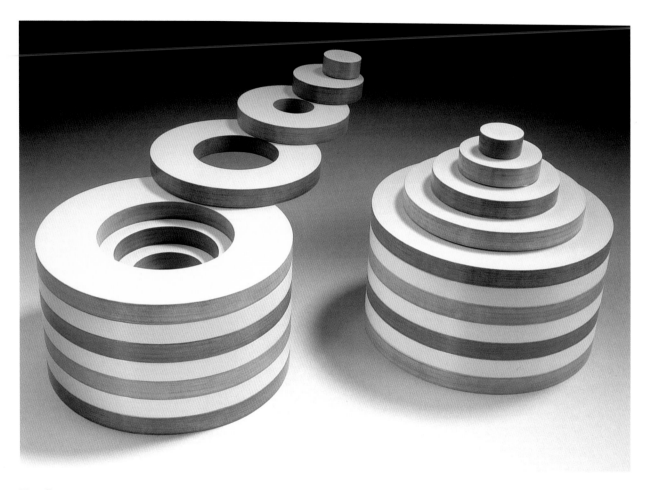

EMI OZAWA
Wound Up, 2001
5½"H x 6"W x 6"D (14 x 15 x 15 CM)
Apple plywood
PHOTO BY MARK JOHNSTON

This box opens and swirls to a close as you move the top ring sideways.

T. BREEZE VERDANT

Tribute to Magorelle, 1994

5½"H x 12"W x 16"D (14 x 31 x 41 CM)

Walnut, pau ferro, rosewood

PHOTO BY ARTIST

Marquetry

T. BREEZE VERDANT
GMO Daisies, 1993
5½"H x 13"W x 18"D (14 x 33 x 46 CM)
Various woods
PHOTO BY ARTIST

T. Breeze Verdant
Midnight Iris, 2003
2¼"H x 3"w x 7"D (6 x 8 x 18 cm)
Ebony, bubinga, tulip, koto
PHOTO BY ARTIST

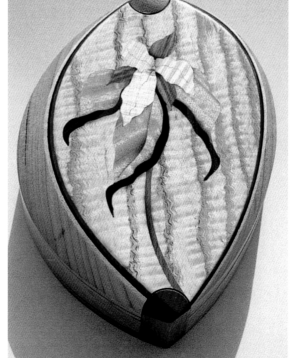

T. Breeze Verdant
Trillium, 2002
2¼"H x 4½"w x 7"D (6 x 12 x 18 cm)
Walnut, bloodwood, Ceylonese satinwood,
tulip, rosewood
PHOTO BY ARTIST

T. BREEZE VERDANT
Magnolia on Rosewood, 2003
3"H X 4"W X 7"D (8 X 10 X 18 CM)
Walnut, bloodwood, rosewood, tulip, holly,
black limba, koto
PHOTO BY ARTIST

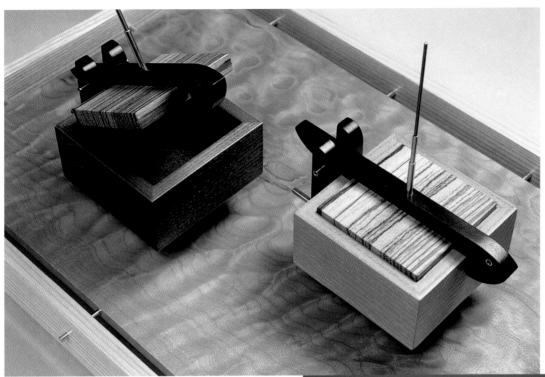

GORDON GALENZA
Hot-rod Alien Boxfish
Cruising to Atlantis, 2002
11¾"H x 20½"W x 11"D (30 x 52 x 28 cm)
Ash, quilted maple, zebrano, ebony,
aluminum, brass, copper, steel, stainless steel,
titanium, fabric

PHOTOS BY JOHN DEAN PHOTOGRAPHS, INC.

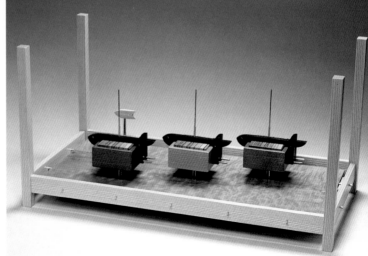

CHRISTOPHER M. VANCE

CHRISTOPHER M. VANCE
In the Weeds
6¾"H x 12½"W x 6"D
(17 x 32 x 15CM)
Wood, copper, gold leaf,
Bakelite
PHOTO BY KOICHI STUDIO

CHRISTOPHER M. VANCE
Insulator, 2002
5¼"H x 10"W x 5¼"D
(14 x 26 x 14 CM)
Wood, gold-plated brass,
ceramic electrical insulator
PHOTO BY KOICHI STUDIO

THOMAS RAUSCHKE &
KAAREN WIKEN

THOMAS RAUSCHKE AND KAAREN WIKEN
Box Turtle Box, 2002
5½"H x 7"W (14 x 18 cm)
Hardwoods, glass, cotton floss
PHOTOS BY WILLIAM LEMKE

Thomas Rauschke and Kaaren Wiken
Dragon Castle, 2001
25"h (69 cm)
Black walnut, various hardwoods, glass, cotton floss
PHOTOS BY WILLIAM LEMKE

THOMAS RAUSCHKE AND KAAREN WIKEN
Landscape Table, 1998
35"H x 10"W x 18"D (89 x 26 x 46 CM)
Various hardwoods, cotton floss
PHOTO BY WILLIAM LEMKE

TRAVIS TOWNSEND
Place Marker, 1998
33"H X 13"W X 8"D (84 X 33 X 21 CM)
Poplar, maple
PHOTOS BY TAYLOR DABNEY

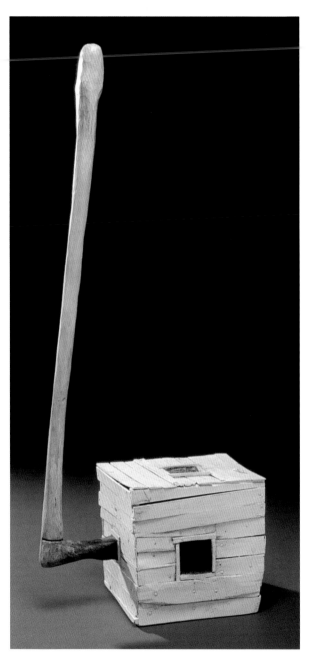

TRAVIS TOWNSEND
New Marooning, 1999-2002
14"H X 26"W X 27"D (36 X 66 X 69 CM)
Poplar, paper
PHOTOS BY TAYLOR DABNEY

257

PAULA COOPERRIDER

PAULA COOPERRIDER
Clouds' Illusions, 1996
6"H x 13"w x 9"D (15 x 33 x 23 CM)
Walnut, leather
PHOTOS BY RUSS GOOD

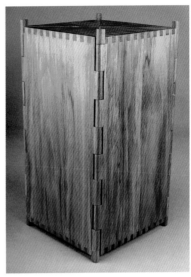

PAULA COOPERRIDER
Campaign Chest, 1995
14"H X 7"W X 7"D
(36 X 18 X 18 CM)
Ipe, pigskin
PHOTOS BY RUSS GOOD

PAULA COOPERRIDER
Unsung Symphony
5"H X 12"W X 13"D
(13 X 31 X 33 CM)
Walnut, leather, found objects
PHOTO BY NEIL COOPERRIDER

EDWARD TEASDALE

EDWARD TEASDALE
Chest (5 lids)
54"H x 18¾"W x 20¼"D (137 x 48 x 52 CM)
Reclaimed wood
PHOTO BY ARTIST

EDWARD TEASDALE
Chest (3 lids)
71"H x 13½"W x 14¾"D (181 x 35 x 38 cm)
Reclaimed wood
PHOTO BY ARTIST

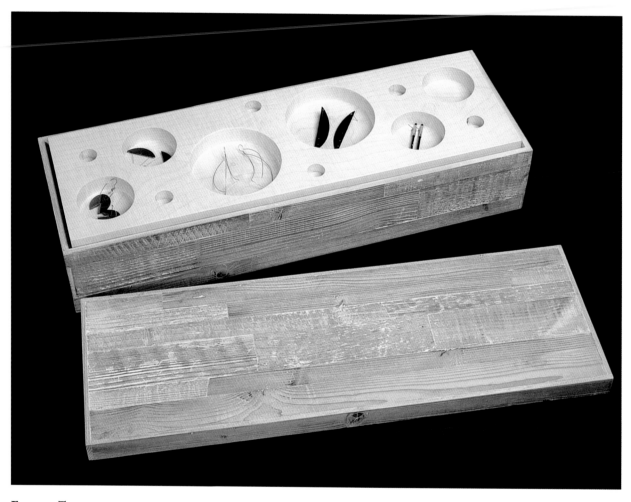

EDWARD TEASDALE
Jewelry Box (3 trays)
15"H X 7¼"W X 6"D (38 X 19 X 15 CM)
Sycamore, reclaimed wood
PHOTO BY ARTIST

CHRISTINE M. ENOS
Beach Case, 1997-1999
12"H x 6"W x 6"D (30 x 15 x 15 CM)
Poplar, found objects, photographs
PHOTOS BY MICHAEL JAMES

263

CHRISTINE M. ENOS
For My Daughter, 1997-1999
11"H x 7"W x 8"D (28 x 18 x 20 CM)
Beech, found objects, photographs
PHOTOS BY MICHAEL JAMES

CHRISTINE M. ENOS
Wedding Box, 1997-1999
6"H x 9"W x 9"D (15 x 23 x 23 CM)
Bass, found objects, photographs
PHOTOS BY MICHAEL JAMES

CHRISTINE M. ENOS
Bond, Union, Tie, 1997-1999
20"H X 9"W X 9"D (51 X 23 X 23 CM)
Poplar, found objects, photographs
PHOTOS BY MICHAEL JAMES

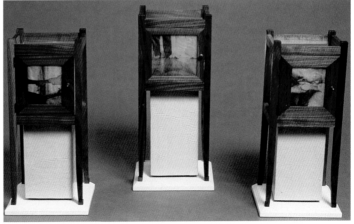

CHRISTINE M. ENOS
For My Daughter, 1997-1999
11"H X 7"W X 8"D (28 X 18 X 20 CM)
Beech, found objects, photographs
PHOTOS BY MICHAEL JAMES

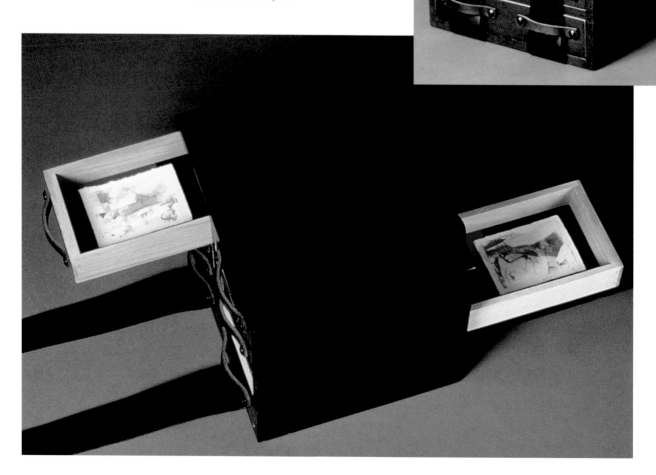

BILL AND NAN BOLSTAD
Jewelry Chest with Six Drawers
15"H x 8"W x 26"D (38 x 21 x 66 CM)
Western maple
PHOTO BY ARTISTS

BILL AND NAN BOLSTAD
Three-drawer Lift-top Jewelry Chest
15"H x 9"W x 10"D (38 x 23 x 26 CM)
Maple, bird's-eye maple
PHOTO BY ARTISTS

JENNIFER ANDERSON
Ellipse, 2000
11½"H X 10"W X 9"D
(29 X 26 X 23 CM)
Pear, machiche
PHOTOS BY JASON ANDERSON

PETER COOK

Lines of Containment III, 2001
9"H X 4"W X 4"D (23 X 10 X 10 CM)
Jarrah, blackbutt, acacia, sterling silver,
stainless steel, brass, nylon
PHOTOS BY TIM LOFTHOUSE

PETER COOK

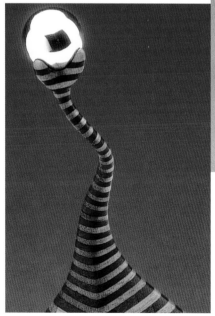

This box, third in a limited edition of four,
features a concealed locking mechanism hidden
within the form.

PETER COOK

Diamond Box, 2000

2¼"H x 4¾"w x 6"D (6 x 12 x 15 CM)

West Australian marri, camphor laurel, Balinese macassar ebony, sterling silver

PHOTOS BY VICTOR FRANCE

PETER COOK

Gold Box, 1998

4"H x 11"w x 7¾"D (10 x 28 x 20 CM)

Jarrah, red morrell, sandalwood, jam, ebony, yellow tingle, sterling silver, brass, spring steel

PHOTO BY VICTOR FRANCE

This is a cremation urn.

JACK AND LINDA FIFIELD
Heaven and Earth, 1997
8"H X 8"W X 8"D (21 X 21 X 21 CM)
Maple box, walnut and cocobolo lid, ebony pins,
Czecholosvakian glass beads, nylon thread
PHOTO BY JACK FIFIELD

JACK FIFIELD
Black Tree, 2001
5"H x 8"W x 8"D (13 x 21 x 21 cm)
Maple, African blackwood
PHOTO BY ARTIST

BENJAMIN J. BLANC

BENJAMIN J. BLANC
The Travelling Show, 2003
6"H X 4½"W X 4½"D (15 X 12 X 12 CM)
Basswood, plastic
PHOTOS BY MARK JOHNSTON

JOAN CARSON
Poof, 1997
18"H X 5"W X 5"D (46 X 13 X 13 CM)
Pine, fabric, fiber reactive dye
PHOTO BY WAYNE HARRIMAN

The wood was first made into a wheelchair ramp for my father when I was taking care of him after a stroke; then some of the wood was made into a cart to haul a large horse sculpture around. Finally, the wood and wheels went to make the Yardstick Box.

MILES R. JOHNSON
Yardstick Box, 2003
15½"H X 12"W X 12"D
(40 X 31 X 31 CM)
Plywood, yardsticks, screen,
nails, glue, copper, photographs
PHOTO BY ARTIST

GREGORY K. WILLIAMS
Pueblo Deco Chest, 1998
40"H x 16"W x 20"D (102 x 41 x 51 cm)
Red maple, cherry, walnut, red cedar,
butternut, spalted sugar maple
PHOTOS BY JERRY ANTHONY

GREGORY K. WILLIAMS
Post-modern Chest, 1997
18"H X 18"W X 9"D (46 X 46 X 23 CM)
Cherry, walnut, maple, Osage orange
PHOTO BY JERRY ANTHONY

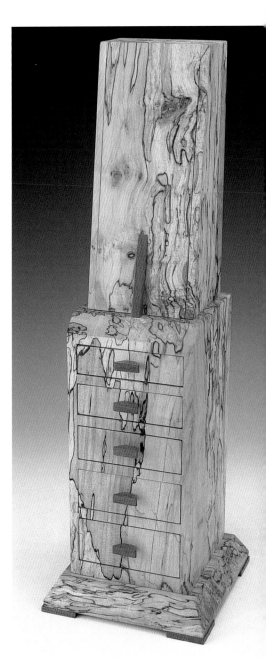

GREGORY K. WILLIAMS
Spalted Tower, 2000
22"H X 8"W X 8"D (56 X 21 X 21 CM)
Spalted silver maple, walnut
PHOTO BY JERRY ANTHONY

GREGORY K. WILLIAMS
Frank, 1999
12"H X 18"W X 18"D (31 X 46 X 46 CM)
Walnut, cherry, butternut, spalted maple
PHOTOS BY JERRY ANTHONY

GREGORY K. WILLIAMS
Gregor's Castle, 1995
36"H x 22"W x 10"D (92 x 56 x 26 CM)
Spalted maple, cherry, walnut, poplar, Osage orange
PHOTOS BY JERRY ANTHONY

MARK REHMAR
Hinged Treasure Box, 2000
4¾"H X 8½"W X 5¼"D
(12 X 22 X 13 CM)
Curly maple, walnut
PHOTO BY GEORGE POST

MARK REHMAR

MARK REHMAR
Watch Winder Box, 2003
8"H X 14"W X 10"D (21 X 36 X 26 CM)
Curly maple, walnut, madrone burl
PHOTO BY ARTIST

MARK REHMAR
His 'n' Her Box, 2002
4"H X 19"W X 8"D (10 X 49 X 21 CM)
Bubinga, redwood burl, wenge
PHOTO BY ROB JAFFE

MARK REHMAR
Silverware Chest with Drawer, 2002
8¾"H x 18¼"W x 15½"D (22 x 47 x 40 CM)
Curly maple, walnut, madrone burl
PHOTO BY ROB JAFFE

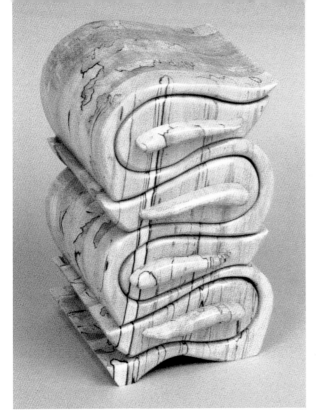

HAROLD D. ENGELKE
Ultimate Curve, 2003
9½"H X 5½"W X 5"D (24 X 14 X 13 CM)
Wood
PHOTO BY ARTIST

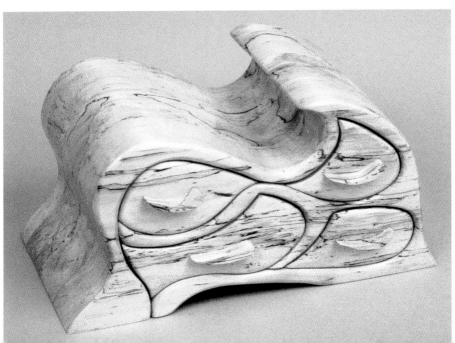

HAROLD D. ENGELKE
Rouge Wave II, 2002
6"H X 12½"W X 6½"D
(15 X 32 X 17 CM)
Wood
PHOTO BY ARTIST

HAROLD D. ENGELKE
Dave's Box, 2002
10"H x 4"w x 4"D (26 x 10 x 10 CM)
Wood
PHOTO BY ARTIST.

HAROLD D. ENGELKE
Flower, 2002
9½"H x 7"w x 5"D
(24 x 18 x 13 CM)
Wood
PHOTO BY ARTIST.

HAROLD D. ENGELKE
Dark Tower, 2002
16"H x 4"W x 4"D (41 x 10 x 10 CM)
Wood
PHOTO BY ARTIST

ROBERT GRUNDMAN
Regency Basket-weave Jewelry Case, 1998
5½"H x 12½"w x 8½"D (14 x 32 x 22 cm)
Koa
PHOTO BY JOHN BAGLEY

ROBERT GRUNDMAN

ROBERT GRUNDMAN
Medium Koa Jewelry Box, 1996
4½"H x 12¼"w x 7½"D (12 x 31 x 19 cm)
Koa, Indian rosewood
PHOTO BY JOHN BAGLEY

DAVID SENGEL
A Turtle Named Speedy, 1999
2"H X 5"W (5 X 13 CM)
Ebonized pear, rose thorns
PHOTO BY MICHAEL SIEDE

This box's bottom shell pulls off to reveal a hollow interior.

DAVID SENGEL
Cyclops Box, 2000
2½"H x 5"W (7 x 13 CM)
Chinaberry wood, hercules club thorns, magnifying lens

PHOTO BY MICHAEL SIEDE

Collection of John Cram

DAVID SENGEL,
Ritual Shedding of Thorns, 2000
7"H x 5"W (18 x 13 CM)
Pear, cherry burl, rose thorns, porcelain
PHOTO BY MICHAEL SIEDE

Turned, carved, sandblasted, dyed.
The hands are porcelain.

MICHAEL MODE

MICHAEL MODE
Akbar's Accolade, 1996
17½"H X 11½"W (45 X 29 CM)
Curly maple, bloodwood, holly,
ebony, pink ivory, goncalo alves
PHOTO BY BOB BARRETT

MICHAEL MODE
Ululation of the Twelve, 1997
17"H x 13"W (43 x 33 CM)
Holly, ebony, bubinga, bloodwood
PHOTOS BY LARRY SANDERS

MICHAEL MODE
The Point of Wings, 2002
9¾"H x 17"W x 8½"D (25 x 43 x 22 CM)
Holly, ebony, bubinga, bloodwood
PHOTO BY ALEX WILLIAMS

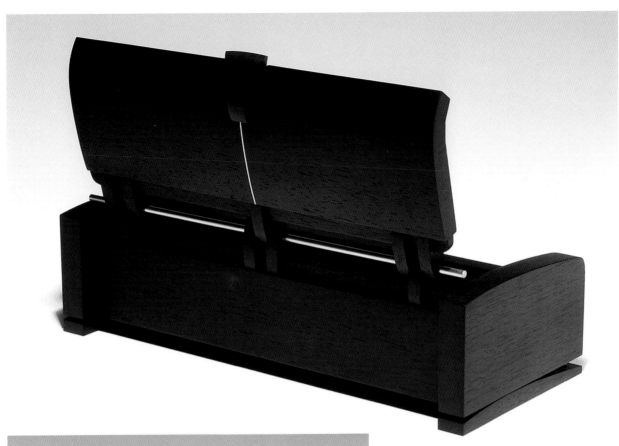

PHILIP WEBER
On Firm Ground, 2003
2"H X 6½"W X 2¾"D (5 X 17 X 6 CM)
Ebony, sterling silver
PHOTOS BY ARTIST

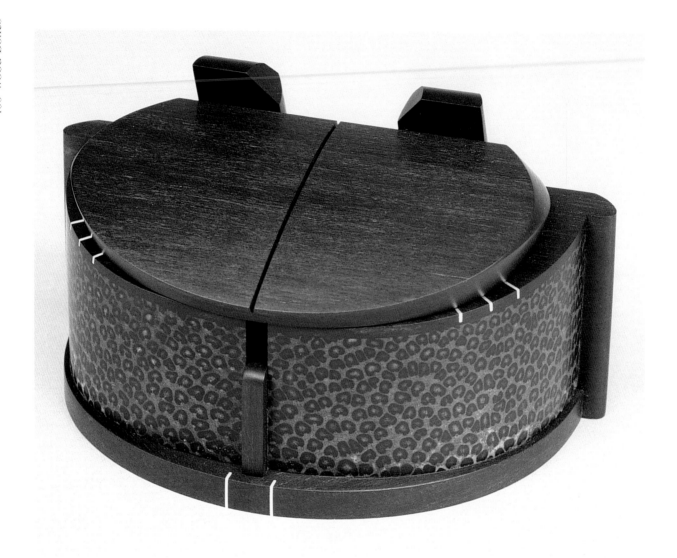

PHILIP WEBER
Leopard, 1999
2¼"H X 3½"W X 3"D (6 X 9 X 8 CM)
Ebony, silver, black palm
PHOTO BY ARTIST

PHILIP WEBER
Big Swing, 2000
2¼"H x 5½"w x 1¾"D (6 x 14 x 4 CM)
Ebony, leopardwood, brass
PHOTOS BY ARTIST

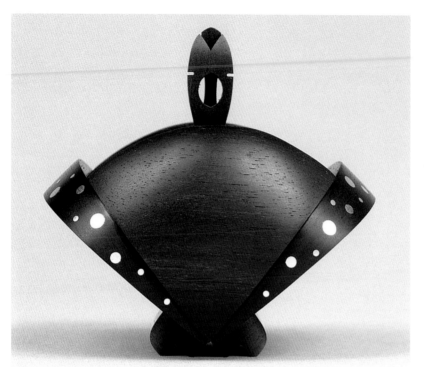

PHILIP WEBER
Molten, 2001
2¼"H x 2½"W x 2¼"D (6 x 7 x 6 CM)
Ebony, sterling silver
PHOTO BY ARTIST

Tongue and groove handle

PHILIP WEBER
Ruckus, 2001
1¾"H x 5¾"W x 2¼"D
(4 x 15 x 6 CM)
Ebony, silver, Pacific yew
PHOTO BY ARTIST

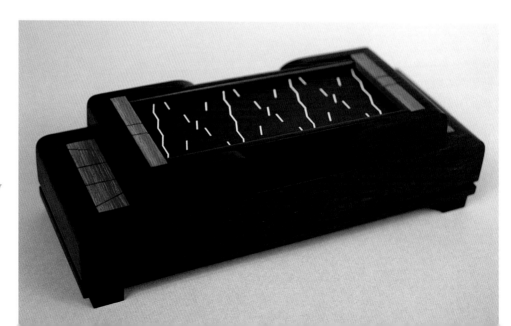

ERVIN SOMOGYI
Kells Zoomorphic Box, 2002
4½"H x 12"W x 8"D (12 x 31 x 21 CM)
Maple, spruce
PHOTO BY GEORGE POST

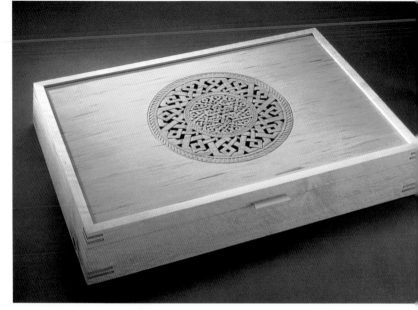

ERVIN SOMOGYI
Venere Shield, 1999
4½"H X 14"W X 9"D
(12 X 36 X 23 CM)
Maple, cedar
PHOTO BY GEORGE POST

ERVIN SOMOGYI
Celtic Knotwork Panel Box, 1996
4"H X 12"W X 8"D (10 X 31 X 21 CM)
Maple, spruce
PHOTO BY GEORGE POST

ERVIN SOMOGYI
*Music Box with Star of Bokhour Design
and Music Movement,* 1996
5½"H x 9"W x 5"D (14 x 23 x 13 CM)
Maple, spruce, musical movement
PHOTO BY GEORGE POST

TERRY EVANS

TERRY EVANS
Container, 2002
20"H X 8"W X 6"D
(51 X 21 X 15 CM)
Lacewood, hackberry,
bloodwood, Ebon-x
PHOTO BY ARTIST

TERRY EVANS
Jewelry Box, 2002
10½"H x 7"W x 3"D (27 x 18 x 8 CM)
Figured maple, various hardwoods, Ebon-x
PHOTO BY AL SURRATT

TERRY EVANS
Container, 2002
9½"H x 8½"W x 6"D (24 x 22 x 15 CM)
Bloodwood, ash, Ebon-x
PHOTO BY AL SURRATT

RUSSELL GREENSLADE
Toucan Box, 2003
9"H x 5"W x 14"D (23 x 13 x 36 CM)
Basswood
PHOTO BY DENNIS GORDON

RUSSELL GREENSLADE

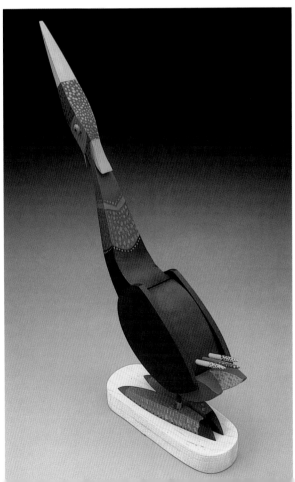

RUSSELL GREENSLADE
Cormorant Box, 2003
14"H x 4"W x 8"D (36 x 10 x 21 CM)
Basswood
PHOTO BY DENNIS GORDON

RUSSELL GREENSLADE
Partridge Box, 2002
6"H X 4"W X 8"D (15 X 10 X 21 CM)
Walnut, cherry
PHOTO BY DENNIS GORDON

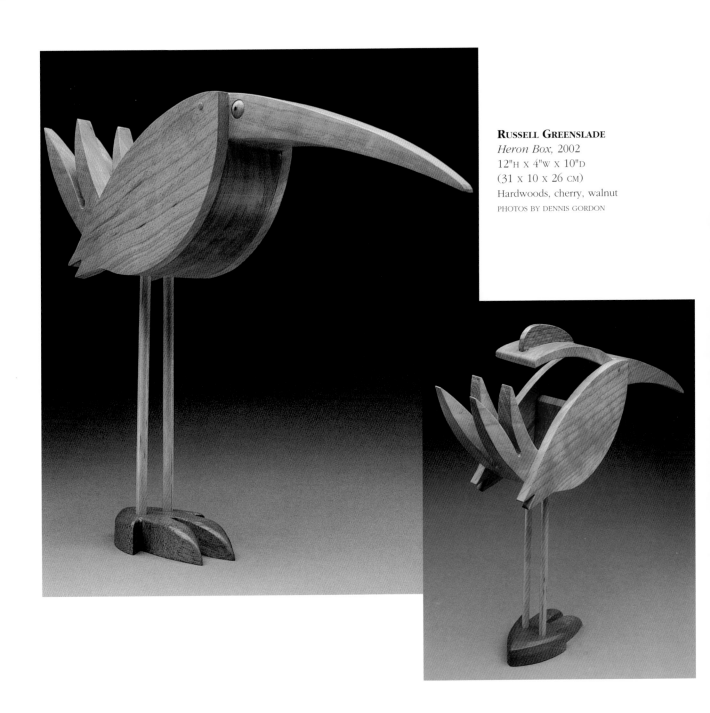

RUSSELL GREENSLADE
Heron Box, 2002
12"H X 4"W X 10"D
(31 X 10 X 26 CM)
Hardwoods, cherry, walnut
PHOTOS BY DENNIS GORDON

305

ROY J. TSUMOTO

ROY J. TSUMOTO
Matched Compression Curly Koa Jewelry Box, 2003
8"H x 20"W x 10"D (21 x 51 x 26 CM)
Koa
PHOTOS BY HUGO DEVRIES

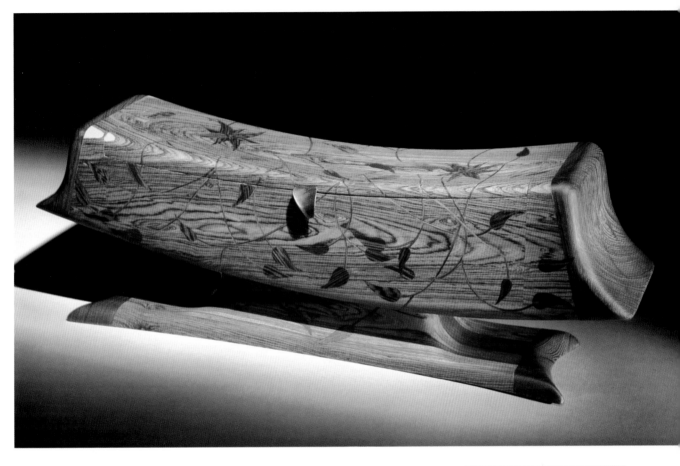

PETER SCHLECH
Autumn Leaves, 1998
5¾"H X 20"W X 8"D (15 X 51 X 21 CM)
Bacote, ziricote
PHOTO BY ARTIST

PETER SCHLECH

*This box features 15 coats of rubbed lacquer and
35 inlays of vines and leaves.*

PETER SCHLECH
Shinto Series #5, 2000
9½"H x 18"W x 5"D (24 x 46 x 13 CM)
Quilted maple, spalted maple, ziricote
PHOTO BY ARTIST

*This box features all bandsawn handshaping,
through-mortise joinery, and four bookmatched
drawers curved in three dimensions.*

PETER SCHLECH
Arched Top Chest, 1999
18"H X 23"W X 12"D (46 X 59 X 31 CM)
Sapele, ebony
PHOTOS BY ARTIST

TERRI L. CADMAN
Mother and Child, 2001
7"H x 14"W x 9"D (18 x 36 x 23 CM)
Curly maple, cherry
PHOTOS BY ARTIST

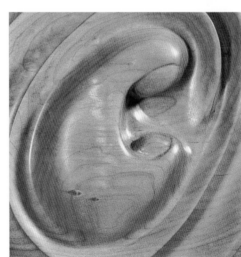

BRIAN F. HABERMAN
False Start, 2003
11"H x 16"W x 14"D (28 x 41 x 36 CM)
Poplar, cherry
PHOTOS BY ARTIST

BRIAN F. HABERMAN
Urn, 2002
12"H x 7"W x 7"D (31 x 18 x 18 CM)
Poplar
PHOTO BY ARTIST

BRIAN F. HABERMAN
Urn, 2002
12"H x 7"W x 7"D AND 10"H x 7"W x 7"D
(31 x 26 x 27 CM AND 26 x 18 x 18 CM)
Walnut
PHOTO BY ARTIST

JAKE ANTONELLI
Laptop, 2001
12"H x 10"W x 11"D (31 x 26 x 28 CM)
Wenge, mahogany, inlaid silver
PHOTO BY MARK JONSTON

JAKE ANTONELLI

This box was inspired by penmanship, which preceded digital communication

JAKE ANTONELLI
Teaboxes, 2003
4"H X 4"W X 8"D (10 X 10 X 21 CM)
Cherry, Korean cashew paint
PHOTOS BY MARK JONSTON

JAKE ANTONELLI
Urns, 2003
4"H X 4"W X 9"D (10 X 10 X 23 CM)
Cherry, Korean cashew paint
PHOTOS BY MARK JONSTON

*This box was inspired by
commemorations of the deceased.*

NEIL KAGAN

NEIL KAGAN
Rose Box, 2002
3" x 2½" (8 x 7 cm)
Mahogany, basswood
PHOTOS BY ARTIST

NEIL KAGAN
Heart Box, 2002
2"H x 6"W x 6"D (5 x 15 x 15 CM)
Zebrawood
PHOTOS BY ARTIST

JAY AND JANET O'ROURKE
Offering of Love, 2003
25"H x 12"W x 6"D (69 x 31 x 15 CM)
Ebony, pink ivory, rose quartz
PHOTO BY GEORGE POST

JAY AND JANET O'ROURKE
Bird in Flight, 1999
Cocobolo, ebony, tagua nut,
moonstones
PHOTO BY GEORGE POST

JAY AND JANET O'ROURKE
Hinged Box Series, 1968-2003
SMALLEST 1⅜"H X 1⅜"W X 1¾"D;
LARGEST 5"H X 4¼"W X 1¾"D (CM)
Various woods
PHOTO BY GEORGE POST

Their signature look

EUGENE WATSON
Ziggurat Box, 1995
8"H X 10"W X 10"D (21 X 26 X 26 CM)
Figured maple, abalone
PHOTO BY JOHN BEDESSEM

Eugene Watson
Tri-Box, 2001
5"H X 15"W X 15"D (13 X 38 X 38 CM)
Zircote, curly koa, abalone
PHOTOS BY JOHN BEDESSEM

EUGENE WATSON

Trapezoid Box, 2000

8½"H x 9"W x 9"D (22 x 23 x 23 cm)

Bubinga, maple

PHOTOS BY JOHN BEDESSEM

Jonathan Pressler

Jonathan Pressler
Ceremonial Vessels, 1995
44½"H x 11½"W x 11½"D (113 x 29 x 29 cm)
Bubinga, curly maple, pear, purpleheart, Baltic birch, brass
PHOTO BY ROB STANTON

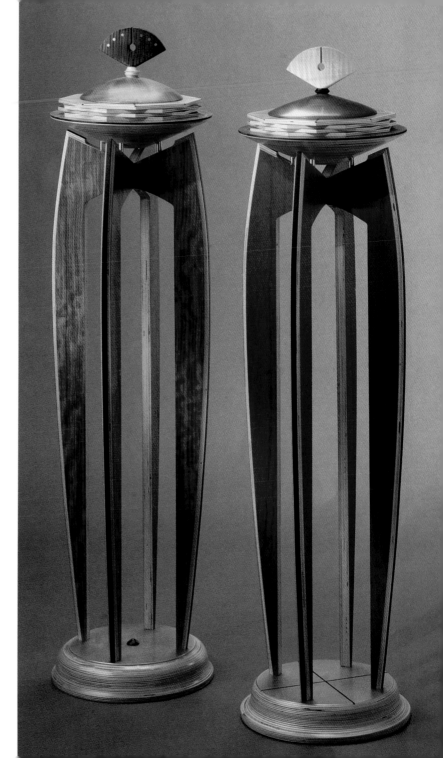

JONATHAN PRESSLER
Temple of Artemis, 1996
11"H x 9½"W x 9½"D (28 x 24 x 24 CM)
Bubinga, curly maple, obeche, brass

JONATHAN PRESSLER
Reliquary, 1995
9½"H x 12"W x 12"D (24 x 31 x 31 CM)
Bubinga, curly maple, Baltic birch
plywood, brass

JONATHAN PRESSLER
Vessel in Search of a Ritual, 1995
9½"H x 12"W x 12"D (24.1 x 31 x 31 CM)
Purpleheart, curly maple, pear, Baltic birch
PHOTOS BY ARTIST

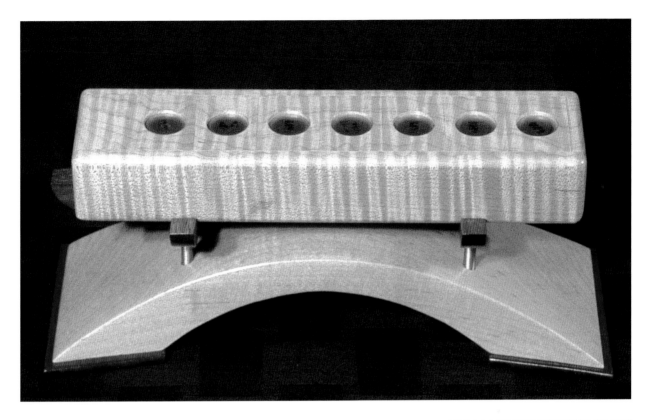

JONATHAN PRESSLER
This is Your Mind on Drugs, 2002
1"H X 6½"W X 1½"D (3 X 17 X 4 CM);
ON ALTAR, TOTAL MEASUREMENT IS
3½"H X 7¼"W X 3"D (9 X 19 X 8 CM)
Curly maple, purpleheart, brass
PHOTOS BY ARTIST

*This box serves as an elegant, practical
alternative to the plastic pillboxes, designed to
hold seven days' worth of pills.*

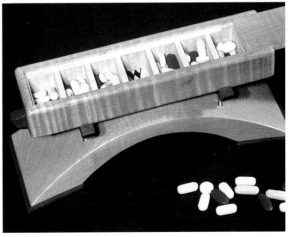

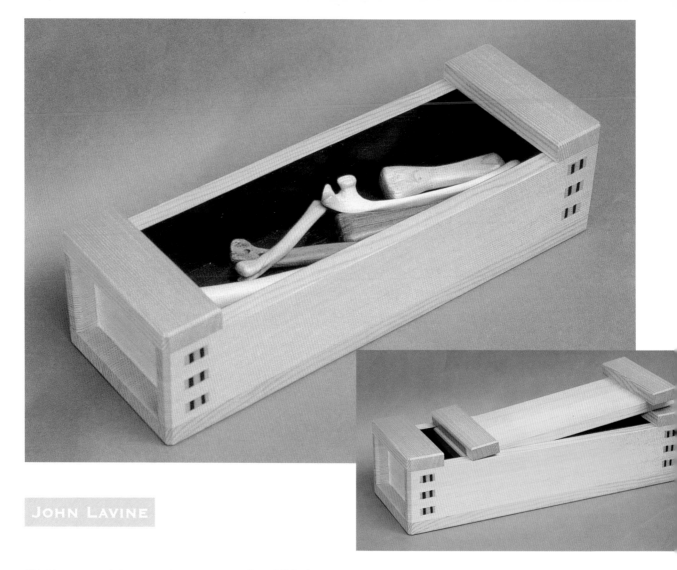

JOHN LAVINE

This piece was made in response to a news report that a bill had been introduced into Congress to log the Tsongas National Forest in southeastern Alaska. The box is made of recycled old-growth Douglas fir and Ebon-x, a substitute for real (and endangered) ebony; the "bones" are carved from scraps of three cedar types native to the Pacific Northwest. All these woods are over-logged.

JOHN LAVINE
Reliquary I (for the Tsongas), 1998
3"H x 12"W x 4"D (8 x 31 x 10 CM)
Recycled Douglas fir, Western red cedar, Alaska yellow cedar, Port Orford cedar, Ebon-x
PHOTOS BY ARTIST

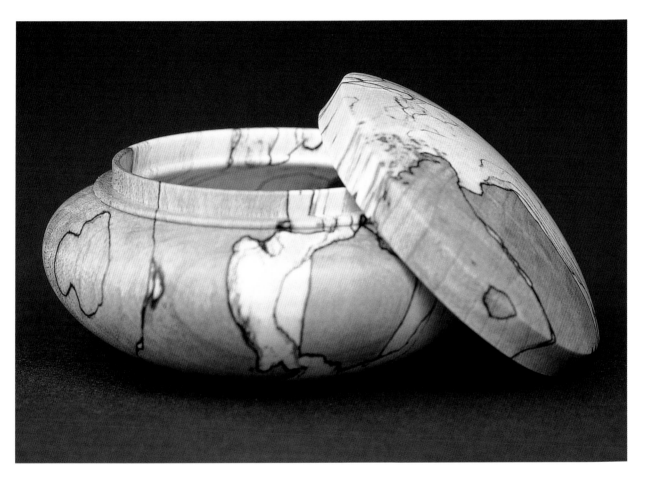

KIP CHRISTENSEN
Lidded Container, 1998
2½"H X 3½" DIAMETER
Spalted maple
PHOTO BY PHOTO CRAFT, OREM, UTAH

KIP CHRISTENSEN
Lidded Jewelry Box, 1999
2"H x 3½" DIAMETER
Elk antler, Pink ivory, turquoise
PHOTOS BY PHOTO CRAFT, OREM, UTAH

ANDREW COSTINE
The Screamer, 1999
8"H x 20"W x 10"D (21 x 51 x 26 CM)
Curly maple, rosewood
PHOTOS BY CHRIS BARTOL

Carved with an auto body grinder.

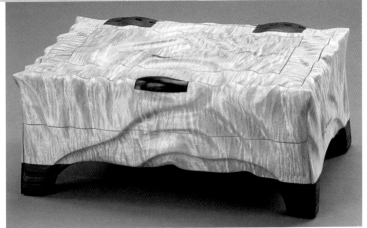

ANDREW COSTINE
Chest, 2002
15"H X 12"W X 14"D (38 X 31 X 36 CM)
Quilted maple, rosewood
PHOTO BY JERRY ANTHONY

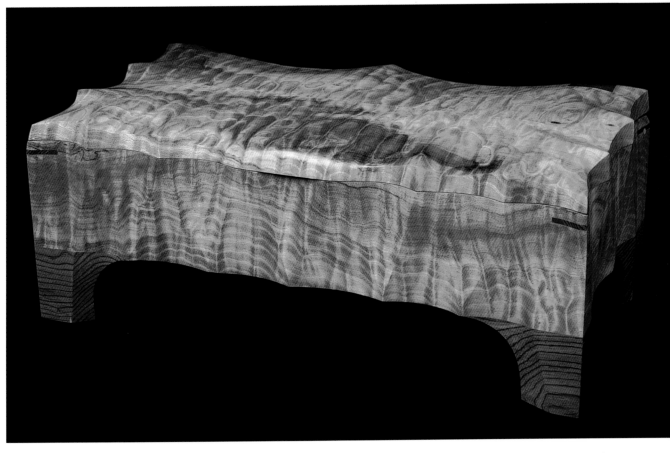

ANDREW COSTINE
Jewelry Chest, 2000
7¾"H X 10"W X 9"D (20 X 26 X 23 CM)
Redheart, quilted maple
PHOTO BY CHRIS BARTOL

The hinges are wooden.

GARY UPTON
Jewelry Chest, 1994
4"H X 16"W X 8"D (10 X 40.5 X 20.5 CM)
Walnut, maple, bubinga, zirocote, bocote,
tulip, rosewood

PHOTO BY JAMES MARKS

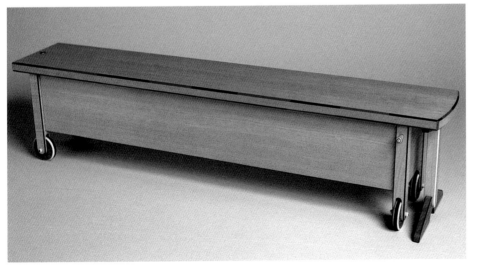

TOM LOESER
Box with Stuck Lid, 1994
5"H x 22"W x 4"D
(13 x 56 x 10.2 CM)
Sitka spruce, mahogany,
maple
PHOTOS BY ARTIST

TOM LOESER
Box 3³, 1996
12"H x 24"W x 7"D (31 x 61 x 18 CM)
Mahogany
PHOTOS BY ARTIST

TOM LOESER
Dovetail Box, 1991
14"H X 23"W X 14"D (36 X 59 X 36 CM)
Corrugated paper, colored paper
PHOTO BY ARTIST

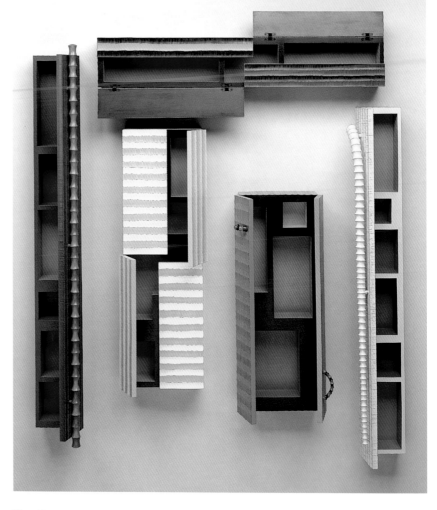

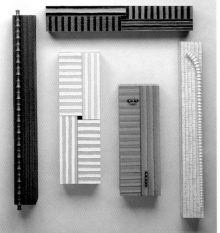

TOM LOESER
(clockwise from top)
Horizontal Square; Bone; Ambidextrous; Vertical Square; Stretch; 2002
42"H x 6"w x 5 1/2"D (107 x 15 x 14 cm); 48"H x 6"w x 5½"D (122 x 15 x 14 cm);
30"H x 11"w x 5½"D (76 x 28 x 14 cm); 36"H x 11"w x 5½"D (92 x 28 x 14 cm);
54"H x 6"w x 5½"D (137 x 15 x 14 cm)
Mahogany

PHOTOS BY BILL LEMKE

WIL AND LIN CHRISTOPHER
Rabbit, 2003
8"H X 12"W X 6"D (20.3 X 31 X 15.2 CM)
Poplar
PHOTO BY MAX ANTON BIRNKAMER

WIL & LIN CHRISTOPHER

WIL AND LIN CHRISTOPHER
Wave, 2002
11"h x 13"w x 10"d (28 x 33 x 25.4 cm)
Poplar
PHOTO BY MAX ANTON BIRNKAMER

WIL AND LIN CHRISTOPHER
Basket, 2003
17"H x 8"W x 6"D (43 x 20 x 15 CM)
Poplar, maple burl, forged copper,
etched brass
PHOTOS BY MAX ANTON BIRNKAMER

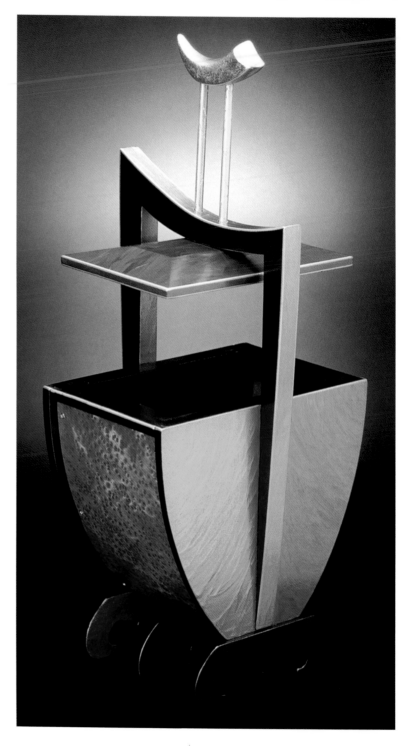

WIL AND LIN CHRISTOPHER
Starship, 1999
16"H X 8"W X 8"D
(41 X 20.3 X 20.3 CM)
Poplar
PHOTO BY STUDIO III

WIL AND LIN CHRISTOPHER
Googi, 1998
8"H x 14"W x 6"D (20 x 36 x 15 CM)
Poplar
PHOTO BY STUDIO III

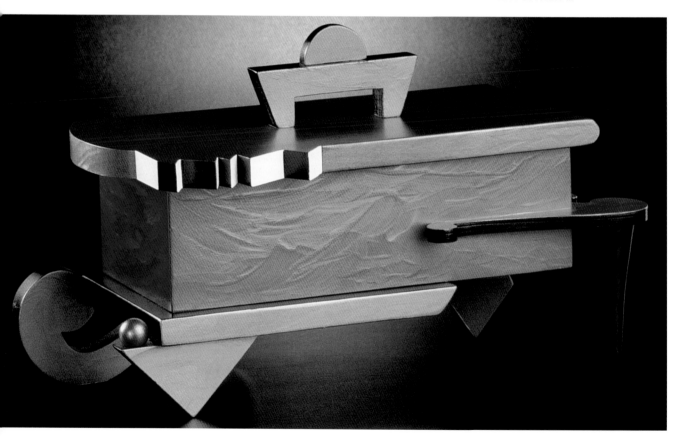

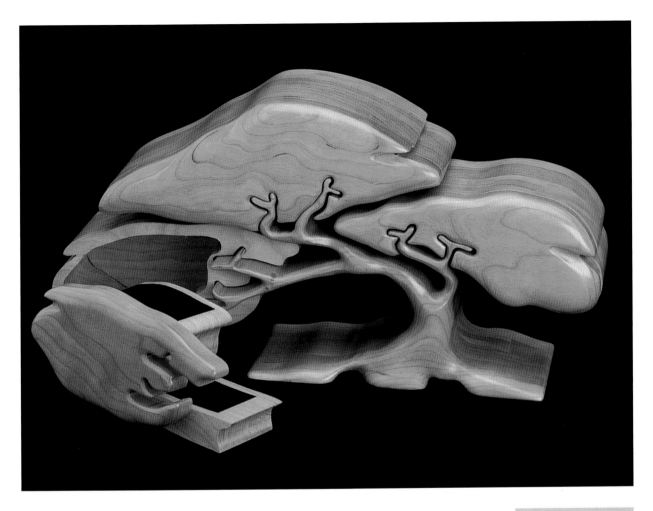

DAVID ROSS
Untitled, 2000
6½"H x 13½"W x 3¼"D (17 x 34.3 x 8 CM)
Cherry
PHOTO BY JAMES KING

DAVID ROSS
Untitled, 2001
9¾"H X 16"W X 4"D (25 X 41 X 10.2 CM)
Bird's-eye maple
PHOTO BY JAMES KING

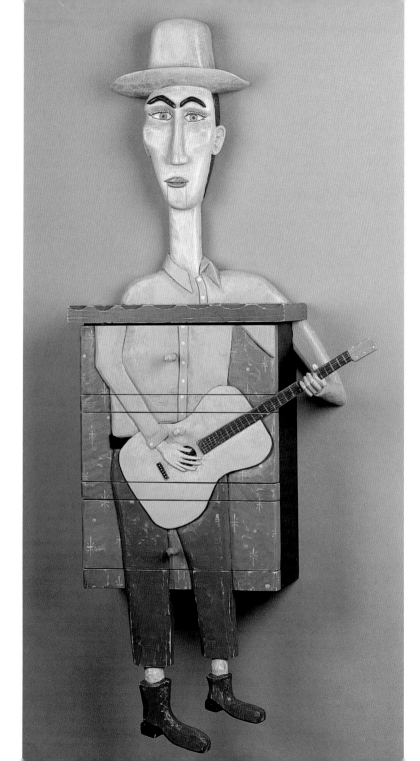

TOM HANEY
Red, 2003
32"H x 13½"w x 5½"D
(81.2 x 34.3 x 14 CM)
Basswood, pine
PHOTO BY DAVIES AND LAWERY

*In each of the following boxes, the bottom
drawer operates the mouth, the middle drawer
operates the eyes, and the top drawer operates
the eyebrows.*

345

TOM HANEY
Queen of Diamonds, 2003
32"H X 10"W X 5½"D (81.2 X 25.4 X 14 CM)
Basswood, pine
PHOTO BY DAVIES AND LAWERY

TOM HANEY
A Hand to Hold, 2001
26"H X 8½"W X 4¼"D (66 X 22 X 11 CM)
Basswood, pine
PHOTO BY GREG CAMPBELL

TOM HANEY
Polka King, 2000
29"H x 8½"W x 4¾"D (74 x 22 x 12 CM)
Basswood, pine
PHOTO BY BRAD NEWTON

347

ACKNOWLEDGMENTS

Thank you to the hundreds of artists who answered our call for art. We could not have made this book without you.

Thank you Tony Lydgate, for your inestimable skill, humor, and patience. I'm still delighted that you said yes to this book. (I hope you are, too.)

Charlie and Celia, I am grateful to each of you for your collaboration on the design and production. The book looks great. For editorial guidance and support, thank you Deborah and Carol. For scheduling assistance, thank you Todd. You made my life easier.

My colleagues Delores, Rosemary, Jeff, Lorna, Nathalie, Rebecca, and Shannon, and freelance copyeditor and proofreader Marilyn Hastings, were invaluable in the creation of this book. Thank you.

For moral support, I am grateful to Katherine, Rain, Chelsea, and Lauren.

Veronika Alice Gunter, Editor

ARTIST INDEX